PRAISE FOR

Biblical Prosperity and Success
Ruminator Style

I have asked a few people from all walks of life and cultures to read the rough draft of *Biblical Prosperity and Success Ruminator Style* and give me a review. I believe that the principles/laws of God, supernatural and natural, work. These are a few who graciously shared their time and words. I am blessed and encouraged.

I remember when I first read Joshua 1:8 many years ago and the excitement that I felt after reading this incredible promise of God's success and prosperity for those willing to apply it. Rodney Boyd, a dear friend, a discipler of mine, and consummate teacher, digs into the scriptures to offer us a clear understanding of God's principles and promises for Kingdom success and prosperity. Mr. Boyd's passion for helping others develop a mindset that aligns with God's design and will for one's life is a priceless gift to those willing to apply it.
~Michael Priebe Physical Therapy Assistant
Singer/Musician/Recording Artist
Inventor of Memory Peel
CEO of the RelaxStation Company

Rodney Boyd is a multi-talented, anointed teacher and declarer of the Bible. Having known Rodney nearly 23 years, I have had the opportunity and privilege to sit under his teachings weekly for a number of years. He has a deep grasp on the root meaning of the Scriptures and does a thorough job of digging into the root words in the Greek, Aramaic and Hebrew to be properly prepared to share the Word of God accurately. Rodney's writings bring a touch of tongue in cheek humor as well as poignant stories to relate the message the Scriptures are trying to relay in a common man's understanding so that you walk away like a 'ruminant' chewing on the Word of God to digest it into bite sized remnants that you can use and apply to your everyday living.

~Pastor Alan D. Smith
Bachelors Biblical Studies and Ministry
Nation2Nation Christian University
Family Life Pastor, Springhouse Church
Smyrna, Tennessee

Biblical Prosperity and Success is the heartbeat of Rodney Boyd, a friend for nearly fifty years. He writes uniquely and powerfully of his life experience. I know you will learn and grow from the "Ruminator" who loves Jesus and lives out what he teaches. I am blessed to call him a friend and a faithful brother. Thank you for the wisdom and advice you share in your book.

~Paul Bane
Pastor Emeritus, New Hope Community Church
Brentwood, Tennessee

It is my honor to be able to talk about the impact that Rodney Boyd has had and is having on my life through his writings and teachings of The Word of God. He writes and teaches in a way that is so genuine and from the heart. I know for a fact that when he writes, he only desires to write from inspiration of the Holy Spirit and only in a way that is edifying to His Father. In this book you will see this is the heartbeat of Rodney and that his desire truly is for you to live a blessed and prosperous life. I pray that you find his teaching as impactful as I have and that by the end, you too realize the power of God and how we can live a prosperous life like my friend and mentor Rodney Boyd.

~Matthew McCain
President and CEO, M&P Renovation, Inc.

Biblical Prosperity & Success Ruminator Style by Rodney Lewis Boyd should be read by anyone wanting to be successful and fulfilled according to scripture. Mr. Boyd does possess these desires and I would call him very successful. The following scriptures seem to be fitting in how he strives to live his life and teach others. "Blessed is the one who does not walk in step with the wicked or stand in the way that sinners take or sit in the company of mockers, but whose delight is in the law of the Lord, and who meditates on His law day and night. That person is like a tree planted by streams of water, which yields its fruit in season and whose leaf does not wither, whatever they do prospers." (Psalms 1:1-3)

~Debbie Rowland
Retired Senior Vice President, FirstBank
Wife, Mother, Grandmother

As a Ruminator in Uganda, Africa, I am thankful to God for the privilege to review this wonderful book/workbook at this stage. I totally agree with Rodney Boyd about the wisdom and inspirations pinned down in this book, the balanced perspective under which Prosperity and Success have been weighed, broken down while putting God's word at the center of it all.

Surely, true Prosperity and Success can be realized through correctly applying Biblical principles. I am fully persuaded that this book will spread like burning fire and whoever reads these practical avenues and applies them in their day to day lives, drastic prosperity and success will be a must in their lives, families, communities, countries and the entire world for the glory of God.

~Vicent Efumbi
Director and Pastor, Africa Network Mission–Mityana
Co-founder at Hope Initiative Ministries

What can I say about Rodney Lewis Boyd? It has been a privilege to review his new book. A great work in the teachings of our Lord and Savior Jesus Christ. He brings clarity to "The man who walked on the waters." Being a Speech Pathologist he breaks down what we thought we knew. His humor mixed in with his teaching is a wonderful addition to this amazing book. Rodney has been a personal friend of mine since grammar school. The fantastic journey he is on is a tribute to his love of the lord. There is in my opinion, every reader cannot come away with a better understanding of our Heavenly Father. A truly gifted writer and even greater friend. In my opinion this book belongs in every true believers library.

~Allen Flynn
Former Manager of Greyhound Bus
Sales with Coca Cola and Real Estate

This book encompasses many solid biblical pieces of wisdom regarding the appropriate Christian views of prosperity and success. Rodney here shows how God gives us enough for ourselves as well as to help others, and discusses at length "fulfillment," that is, accomplishing God's will for us. He too reviews the preparation and planning for our endeavor, this life of kingdom prosperity, and gives personal testimony, which is as moving in the text as it was when he told me this personally. He further discusses staying positive, while declaring the virtues, values, and mentality necessary for the long haul, as well as how the confusion of our current era attempts to undermine us. His medical and speech expertise are brought into the work consistently, as is his biblical knowledge, to hammer home the points which are necessary to be made.

He discusses the initial plan of God in Eden, and how God's current "paradigm," i.e., His ideal archetypal plan, is to return to, and continue, blessing us, rather than afflicting or cursing us. (And Rodney as always is not one to shy away from politico-culturally sensitive issues!) Even though we have wandered from the initial plan God set up for man in Eden (by our disobeying and dishonoring as well as distrusting God), Rodney reviews how our Lord's ideal prototypical path and its immense blessings can indeed be once again found. He reviews the underlying foundational necessity of communication, as well as prayer, for achieving such biblical prosperity and success. And he discusses our God-given gifts and talents, as well as the attempted interference of Satan, at times, in God's positive "Pro-Vision", as so nicely he terms it.

Additionally, I greatly like the added Hebrew and Greek roots which help show where many of the contextual words in this work come from, as well as the definitions that Rodney supplies.

This book to me reveals that God does indeed desire man to become, and to maintain, success in his lifetime, albeit only in His will, in His timing, and for His glory. While some goals can certainly be attained by man without God, such will in that instance never fulfill us, nor complete the marvelous plan He intends for each one of us, individually! Therefore, until we get ourselves aligned with our loving Creator Father's will and plan, we shall never achieve the full measure of His intended pending waterfall of blessings, those which He so greatly desires to bestow upon each of His children!

Thus, I greatly encourage the reading of Rodney's "Biblical Prosperity and Success Ruminator Style" work! Additionally, its insights and questions would be excellent for a Bible study/small group study, as well.

~Paul Buechel, M.D Neurologist
Author, *Rise and Shine, Trailblazer*

Biblical Success and Prosperity Ruminator Style is another must read by Rodney Boyd. I have known and been learning from Rodney for over 30 years. Rodney makes reading about, learning, and studying the Bible easier with his practical writing and teaching methods. His books are relatable because he uses real life examples from his experiences as a husband, father, speech pathologist, Sunday school teacher, and martial arts student. He uses humor, great story telling, analogies, and many more strategies that make biblical principles understandable and applicable to your everyday life. This is another book to add to your collection of go-to books for advice on how to live your life in a Godly manner.

~Alison Payne
BS Elementary & Special Ed
M.Ed. School Counseling
Ed.S School Psychology- Nationally Certified School Psych
Realtor, New Construction
At Home With Diversity Certified

Prosperity and success are the American Way! The USA has always been a land of opportunity for those born as American citizens and the millions of immigrants who made their way to America's shores and borders. For many, prosperity and success (by whatever definition an individual claimed) came from self-made plans fulfilled. But for others, the lack of correct teaching on just what IS prosperity and success causes disappointment and unfulfilled expectations.

Now, however, in his book, "Biblical Prosperity And Success Ruminator Style," Rodney Boyd has defined, explained, and set into motion the steps and procedures for finding prosperity and success according to Biblical principles, and it works!

In sixteen chapters, Biblical truths connect with the thread of Scripture from the Old Testament to the New. Plus, the review questions/reminders keep the goals clear, concise, understandable, and attainable; prosperity and success are for the Believer, and the proof is in the reading.

~Jill L. Coble, M.S. Ed.
Teaching Fellow, TN Holocaust Commission

BIBLICAL PROSPERITY AND SUCCESS

Also by
Rodney Lewis Boyd

Never Run a Dead Kata
Written that You may Believe
Pro-Verb Ponderings
Speaking and Hearing the Word of God
Chewing the Daily Cud, Vols 1–4
On Earth as it is in Heaven
How to Live a Maximized Life

BIBLICAL
PROSPERITY
AND
SUCCESS
RUMINATOR STYLE

RODNEY LEWIS BOYD

WordCrafts Press

Biblical Prosperity and Success: Ruminator Style
Copyright © 2023
Rodney Lewis Boyd

ISBN: 978-1-957344-58-4

Cover concept by David Warren.
Cover design by Mike Parker.

Published by WordCrafts Press
Cody, Wyoming 82414
www.wordcrafts.net

To my wife Brenda,
our son Phillip and his wife, Jamie,
and our granddaughter Emerson Grace.

CONTENTS

FOREWORD

I was privileged to be asked to pen a forward to Rodney Lewis Boyd's sequel to *How To Live A Maximized Life*. My only qualification is that I have known Rodney for close to a quarter of a century. During that time his focus to pointing others to the Lord has never wavered. In ***Biblical Prosperity and Success: Ruminator Style***, Rodney continues to blend his varied background with his constantly growing relationship with his Lord and Savior. In the twelve chapters I was honored to preview, he applies decades of being a well-known and highly respected Bible teacher in laying out scriptural principles to be successful and effective while leading a purposeful life.

Rodney touches on his professional background as a speech pathologist, his journey through learning martial arts, his love of family and the Lord, along with the obstacles he has overcome through the power of the Holy Spirit to weave a potential map for the reader. But A map will only get you where you want to go if you are willing to follow the directions. Directions are included.

The world supplies a paint-by-number picture of success and happiness. Rodney Boyd vividly brings to life Biblical principles to chew on—again and again. He celebrates and encourages the reader to have a Christ-like paradigm. If you are not sure what that is, hang-on!

Within these pages you get mentored and motivated by a dedicated and seasoned writer who actively thinks, speaks, writes, and does what determines his life, and discover how you too can achieve success—Ruminator Style.

Michael Hendrickson

INTRODUCTION

This book is about a controversial topic in Christendom—and outside of Christendom—that deals with prosperity and success. On one side of the spectrum you have those who think that it is God's will for you to have lots of cash, fancy cars, large ornate houses, 401(k) plan—in general, *stuff.* On the other side of the spectrum are people who feel that to be truly spiritual you have to be at the poverty level, and if you have not taken a *vow of poverty* then you must be in the flesh (carnal nature).

The hyper-spiritual people who think that their fecal matter (pardon my French), does not stink seem to always be pointing their finger of condemnation at others who don't live the lifestyle that they believe a true Christian should live.

There is one preacher, who we will call *Paul Positive,* that they love to put down. They like to focus on his positive messages, his house size, and the type of car he drives, his fake smile, his hair style, and his trophy wife. They will post a picture of him on social media, standing next to his expensive car with the caption, "Jesus road a donkey and Paul Positive drives an opulent car. I speak to the computer screen and ask them, "Jesus road a donkey, so what model ass are you riding in 2021." If they complain about the size of his house, I point out that I have slept in the Amazon Jungle in a hut on stilts—to avoid the Amazon River overflowing—that has no walls, a thatched roof and a bamboo floor to sleep on. Then I point out to the one complaining that as they live in their modest three bedroom home, with three bathrooms, fully stocked kitchen, air and heat, that to the ones in the Amazon Jungle they are Paul

Positive. It is all about perspective. I could go on and on, but I will cover these and more topics later in this book. Biblical Prosperity and Success Ruminator Style is a collection of teachings, quotes and insights where we will moo, chew and do like a cow chewing its cud.

It is my contention that God's heartbeat is not against success, prosperity, and money but is for us to be stewards of everything He has entrusted us with. After all, it is all His. I define success as *accomplishing the purpose of God in our lives,* and prosperity as *having enough to meet our needs—not our greed—and an overflow to help meet the needs of others.* In a world of socialism, communism, capitalism, and every other kind of –ism there is, the question is not what you've got, but what are you going to do with it?

While we are talking about the Biblical Principles of Prosperity and Success, I would be remiss in not pointing out that just because someone does not have a lot of prosperity or success in the eyes of the world, it does not make them any less prosperous or successful in the eyes of God. I love the Book of Hebrews, chapter eleven that is known theologically as *The Hall of Faith.* It is a list of people who have come and gone before us—aka the cloud of witnesses in Hebrews 12:1—who by faith gained approval and had wonderful (full of wonder) *pro-vision* (positive revelatory insights into God's prosperity and success). But starting in Hebrews 11:36 there is a shift of thought concerning other saints.

> *"And others experienced mockings and scourgings, yes also chains and imprisonment. They were sawn into, they were tempted, they were put to death with the sword; they went about in sheepskins, in goatskins, being destitute afflicted, ill-treated (men of whom the world was not worthy), wandering in deserts and mountains and caves and holes in the ground. AND ALL OF THESE, having gained approval through their faith, DID NOT RECEIVE WHAT WAS PROMISED, because God had provided something better for us, so that they would not be made perfect."*
> ~Hebrews 11:36-40 emphasis mine

These verses do not negate the idea of prosperity and success, but for me, undergirds that fact that no matter what happens, God is in control. I remember being in the Amazon jungle of Peru, and our leader, Bruce Coble, was teaching the tribe on covetnousness. Hey, they did not have anything, but the head of the tribe told Bruce that this was a major problem in the village. When we left, they gave us a chicken, one of their most prized commodities. Fish were everywhere from the river, but they gave us the best they had. I am convinced that they experienced prosperity and success on a level that we never could realize.

Some chapters of this book will be short, while other chapters will be rather lengthy. Some sections will involve merely reading, but others involve homework with questions/answers.

While this book will talk a lot about prosperity and success, be sure that you understand there is an aspect that many *prosperity* believers miss. That is, *the will of God.*

> *Come now, you who say today or tomorrow we will go to such and such a city, and spend a year there and engage in business and make a profit yet you do not know what your life will be like tomorrow, you are just a vapor/mist that appears for a little while and then vanishes away. Instead (of saying you will go to a city, stay a certain amount of time, engage in business and make a profit) you ought to say, IF the Lord wills, we will live and also do this or that.*
> ~James 4:13–15 with additions and emphasis mine
> Ruminator Style

If you don't have the attitude of laying down your plans before Him, then you are boasting, arrogant, evil, (James 4:16)

So, what should you do?

> *Therefore (because of what you just read in James 4:13–15), to the one who knows the right thing to do and does not do it to him it is sin."*
> ~James 4:17

This is the follow-up companion to my previous book called *How To Live A Maximized Lifestyle.*

Be blessed—supremely happy so as to be envied by others as they see you being spiritually prosperous with life-joy and satisfaction in God's favor and salvation, regardless of their outward conditions.

Taken from Jesus' Beatitudes in Matthew 5:1 Amplified Bible

Rodney Lewis Boyd, 2021

CHAPTER ONE

PROSPERITY AND SUCCESS DEFINED

When you hear the words prosperity and success, the mind immediately goes to being number one and wealthy, including cash, homes, cars, stocks and bonds, 401 K, living the good life and being a success accomplishing everything that you do. Of course the good life on the surface may look good, but it ain't always good.

The dictionary definition of prosperity and success is:

PROSPERITY: (1) a successful, flourishing, or thriving condition, especially in financial respects; good fortune. (2) Prosperities, prosperous circumstances, characterized by financial success or good fortune.

~Dictionary.com

SUCCESS: (1) the favorable or prosperous termination of attempts or endeavors; the accomplishment of one's goals. (2) The attainment of wealth, position, honors, or the like. (3) A performance or achievement that is marked by success, as by the attainment of honors (4) a person or thing that has had success, as measured by attainment of goals, wealth.

~Dictionary.com

Earl Nightingale, a motivational speaker from the '50s and '60's defines success, "The progressive realization of a worthy ideal."

Many people strive to win the race, to be successful, to prosper financially, and succeed. The old saying goes, "If you win the Rat Race, you end up being the Number 1 Rat."

Jesus compared the d-evil's intent "to kill, steal, and destroy" (John 10:10) to His own intent "that they may have life and have it (more) abundantly." (John 10:10) Many people live a *good* life but find that it is a poor substitute for *abundant* life.

Wealth seems to be the measuring stick for happiness, but the word *happiness* seems to be obsolete.

WEALTH: (1) a great quantity or store of money, valuable possessions, property, or other riches: (2) an abundance or profusion of anything; plentiful amount: (3) all things that have a monetary or exchange value. (4) Anything that has utility and is capable of being appropriated or exchanged. (5) Rich or valuable contents or produce (6) the state of being rich; prosperity; affluence

Of course, eventually this measuring stick for success and prosperity, if not controlled, will eventually fall short of the mark.

BIBLICAL PROSPERITY AND SUCCESS

PROSPEROUS: tsâlach tsâlêach (tsaw-lakh', tsaw-lay'-akh)=A primitive root; to push forward, in various senses (literally or figuratively, transitively or intransitively): - break out, come (mightily), go over, be good, be meet, be profitable, (cause to, effect, make to, send) prosper (-ity, -ous, -ously).

~Strong's

SUCCESS: śâkal (saw-kal')=A primitive root; to be (causatively make or act) circumspect and hence intelligent: - consider, expert, instruct, prosper, (deal) prudent (-ly), (give) skill (-ful), have good success, teach, (have, make to) understand (-ing), wisdom, (be, behave self, consider, make) wise (-ly), guide wittingly.

~Strong's

These two words are found together in the Biblical book of Joshua..

"This book of the Law shall not depart from your mouth but you

shall meditate on it day and night so that you might be careful to do according to all that is written in it; for then you will make your way prosperous and then you shall have (good) success."

~Joshua 1:8

NOTE: We will discuss this more in the next chapter.
I personally define prosperity and success as:

PROSPERITY: Having enough to meet your needs (not greed) and enough left over to help others.

SUCCESS: Accomplishing the purposes of God in your life.

In our next chapter we will look at Joshua 1:8 and extrapolate the principles,

CHAPTER TWO

JOSHUA 1:8 EXTRAPOLATED

In the last chapter we examined the various definitions of prosperity and success. Now we will look at biblical prosperity and success found in Joshua 1:8.

The children of Israel had just made an amazing journey after being released from Egyptian captivity to a forty-year long journey that should have taken eleven days. (Deuteronomy 1:2) They went from captivity to freedom and back into captivity. They had arrived at their destination, and now they were ready to cross over and possess the Promised Land, a land filled with milk and honey. It is eleven days' journey from Horeb by way of Mount Seir to Kadesh-barnea.

> *"For the children of Israel walked forty years in the wilderness, till all the people who were men of war common folk and women, who came out of Egypt, were consumed, because they did not obey the voice of the LORD—to whom the LORD swore that He would not show them the land which the LORD had sworn to their fathers that He would give us, "a land flowing with milk and honey."*
> ~Joshua 5:6

In the natural eyes, the children of Israel were not prosperous nor were they successful. They were more like failures falling way short of the prosperity level God had in mind for them. The key to Biblical Prosperity and good Success is found in Joshua 1:8.

1. What book did they have at their disposal?
2. What should not happened?

3. Instead of departing from their mouth what should they with it?
4. What must they be careful to do with what was in their mouths?
5. What will they cause and effect be of meditating on the Law day and night?
6. What will they have when they become prosperous?

We can see that there is a direct link to the Law (the Word of God) and prosperity and having (good) success. When it says that it (the Law/Word) "shall not depart from your mouth" that does not mean that you should not speak it (the Law/Word) out loud, but to the contrary. You are to meditate which means to "mutter under your breath."

MEDITATE: hâgâh (haw-gaw')=A primitive root (compare H1901); to murmur (in pleasure or anger); by implication to ponder: - imagine, meditate, mourn, mutter, roar, X sore, speak, study, talk, utter.

~Strong's

RUMINATE: (1) to chew the cud, as a ruminant. (2) To meditate or muse; ponder. (3) to chew again or over and over (4) to meditate on; ponder.

~Dictionary.com

RUMINANT: (1) any even-toed, hoofed mammal of the suborder Ruminantia, being comprised of cloven-hoofed, cud-chewing quadrupeds, and including, besides domestic cattle, bison, buffalo, deer, antelopes, giraffes, camels, and chevrotains. (2) Ruminating; chewing the cud. (3) Contemplative; meditative.

~Dictionary.com)

NOTE: We get the idea of an animal that chews on food, swallows the food that goes through four stomachs/chambers and then regurgitates the food back up in the form of a cud and then chews on the cud giving it the look of a contemplative, meditating animal. The verse could read:

"...but you shall chew the cud in your mouth like a cow or camel, day and night..."

~Joshua 1:8, author's translation

This muttering under the breath the Law (the Word of God) is reminiscent of the Jews at the Wailing Wall where they put rolled up sheets of paper in the wall, and rock back and forth or side to side as they mutter under their breath the Law or prayers.

NOTE: Shuckling (also written as shokeling), from the Yiddish word meaning "to shake" (compare with the German "schaukeln" to swing) is the ritual swaying of worshippers during Jewish prayer, usually forward and back but also from side to side.

To have Biblical Prosperity and Good Success you must meditate/ruminate on the Word day and night. When you leave your prayer position, you don't just turn away, but you turn away to do what is written in the Law/The Word. You must be careful because many pray and forget the *doing* part.

"Faith without corresponding actions (doing) are of none effect."
~James 2:17, Weymouth Translation emphasis mine

Or

"Faith without works is dead."

~James 2:17

Another aspect of prosperity and success is that many people pray to God and then just expect Him to drop the answer down to them. God becomes a magic genie with a lamp to grant their wishes or a cosmic slot machine that you pull His arm for a reward. Joshua 1:8 states, "...for then YOU will make YOUR way prosperous..." You take your faith and put it to work. We will see that the children of Israel (1) Had to cross over (2) Face the giants (3) Possess the Land. Then and only then will they have good success.

The same holds true for us in our ventures (adventures) in attempting to be prosperous and have good success.

CHAPTER THREE

THE PREPARATION FACTOR

For any (Ad)-venture to be successful, you must prepare ahead. The children of Israel and Joshua were told by Moses and God to be "strong and courageous" and to not tremble or be dismayed. I believe they were told this because they were going to have every opportunity to be "weak and discouraged" and every opportunity to shake and quake and look at what they would face wondering why is this happening to us.

Take some time and look up these verses and then determine what they have in common.

1. Deuteronomy 31:6
2. Deuteronomy 31:7
3. Deuteronomy 31:23
4. Joshua 1:6
5. Joshua 1:7
6. Joshua 1:9
7. Joshua 1:18
8. Joshua 10:25

God wanted them to be prepared when they would meet the enemy as they were taking possession of the Promise Land. I think if it was something God gave them, why they would have to be strong and courageous? After all, He did give it to them. I believe that same principle holds as we set out to do anything in our lives— be it business or our daily walk or our spiritual walk.

Another act of preparation is found in the book of Joshua.

"Then Joshua commanded the officers of the people, saying, Pass through the midst of the camp and command the people saying prepare provisions for yourselves, for within three days you are to cross this Jordan, to go in to possess the land which the Lord your God is giving you, to possess it."

~Joshua 1:10

I know whenever I go camping, I don't just hop in the car and drive to the campsite hoping that all the provisions I need will be there. Well, to be honest with you, I don't camp. But I do go to a nice state park and stay at the hotel with all the amenities I need. But if I did go camping, I would make sure I had all the supplies I needed, including the tent, sleeping bags, cots, food, water, protection, mosquito spray, marshmallows, Hershey chocolate bars, graham crackers, and anything else that I could dream up.

NOTE: I have friends who have a nice mobile home that they carry behind their cars and call it *Glamping*—camping in luxury.

I am sure that the children of Israel prepared with everything from swords, slingshots, shields, etc. When we prepare ourselves for warfare (See Ephesians 6:10–19) we make sure the full armor is in place along with being prayed up, the Word, being filled up with the Holy Spirit, forgiveness in our hearts. Why? Because even though we are "in Christ" and Christ is "in us," if we want to be prosperous and have success in our spiritual lives, personal lives, and business lives we must be prepared like a Boy Scout on a mission.

Another aspect of preparation is known as consecration/ sanctification.

"Then Joshua said to the people, consecrate yourselves (today) for tomorrow the Lord will do wonders among you."

~Joshua 3:5 emphasis mine

A lot of times we like to just go with the flow of the Spirit, and whatever happens will happen, and whatever will be will be. We like to call that *sovereignty*, but if you really want to move in the Spirit, you better be prepared. If you are not prepared, the Lord still may move but you will miss it. Did you notice that Joshua (their leader) did not say "let me consecrate you" or "God will consecrate you." He said, "Consecrate yourselves." This speaks of preparation on their part. In business, if you think you will just create a name for your company and the next thing you know you are prosperous and successful, you are only fooling yourselves. I have friends who are very successful business people, and they do not just sit back and wait for the money to flow in. They work it!

I believe that God is in the sanctification and consecration business. In some place in the Bible, *sanctification* and *consecration* appear to be the same thing, but I believe that only God can sanctify someone, set them apart for His purpose, but consecration is what we do in preparation for God to move in our lives. If we attempt to do it ourselves, we end up thinking we have to work our way into a sanctified and consecrated position with the Father. On the other hand, Joshua 3:5 is specific when it says to "consecrate/sanctify yourselves" which makes me think that we have something to do with positioning ourselves for God to do His work in us. While the work done in us is the work done by God, we must approach everything in our lives by faith with the understanding that:

> *"Faith without corresponding actions is of none effect (D.O.A., dead on arrival)."*
> ~James 2:17 Weymouth Translation addition mine
> Ruminator Style)

CHAPTER FOUR

THE RECONNAISANCE REPORT

So far in our look at Biblical Prosperity and Success we have seen the importance of meditating (ruminating) on the Word of God and how important it was to not only think about the Word and speak the Word, but the actual doing of the Word. Then we saw the importance of preparation. Now we look at the importance of the reconnaissance report in having prosperity and success in our quest for the Promise Land. I believe this correlates with scoping out whatever we are attempting to do in our lives and businesses. The children of Israel had a covenant promise from God that was initiated with Abraham, passed on to Moses, Isaac, Jacob (Israel) on down to you and me via faith.

Moses had received marching orders to go into the Promise Land and spy out the land and then come back with a report. Some think that God wanted them to go in and scope out the territory to understand the lay of the land and its inhabitants. I believe that God wanted them to go in and see that what He said was true. I believe we can scope out (go on a reconnaissance mission) in the Word of God to see if what He said was true for anything in our lives.

The Lord was speaking to Moses as he told him to send out men to spy out the land of Canaan which He was giving them. It was not to see if there *was* such a land, but that it was a land that He was giving them. As with most directives from God, there were specifics.

In this case:

1. Spy out the land that He was giving them.

2. Send a man from each of their fathers' tribes (each one was a leader).
3. They were to go up into the Negev, then go up into the hill country.
4. See what the land is like and whether the people who live in it are strong or weak and whether they are few or many.
5. See how is the land in which they live, is it good or bad?
6. See how are the cities in which the live.
7. Are the cities like open camps or with fortifications?
8. How is the land, is it fat or lean?
9. See if there are trees in it or not.
10. Make an effort to get some of the fruit of the land since it was the time of the first ripe grapes.

This was their mission, if they should accept it. Back in the '60s there was a TV show called *Mission Impossible*. The team was given the mission optics that included the disclaimer, "your mission, should you decide to accept it." The tape would self-destruct and the *Mission Impossible* theme music would start to play. Our mission, should we choose to accept it, is called Mission Possible, because as the scripture declares;

   "...with God all things are possible."
   ~Matthew 19:26

They scoped out the land and they cut down a branch with a single cluster of grapes—which they carried on a pole between two men—along with some of the pomegranates and figs. Now that is what I call a fruit basket turn over. It took two men to carry a single cluster of grapes. That is a lot of fine wine and the best grape jelly.

They returned back to base camp after forty days of reconnaissance. They returned to headquarters where Moses and Aaron were waiting. All of the congregation of the sons of Israel were there also. The spies brought back a report and showed them the fruit of the land. They then verified that indeed that the land flowed with milk and honey.

NOTE: Some believe the fruit in the Garden of Eden was *not* an apple but instead was a pomegranate. It has been said that the fruit was originally seedless, but after the fall of Disobedience, after the act of high treason, it was cursed with many seeds. Others say that it *was* an apple, and when the apple was swallowed it lodged in Adam's throat resulting in his Adam's apple, the name for the thyroid notch prominent in males. No one actually knows, but it does make for some fun conjecture.

They started the report with the word, "nevertheless," (Numbers 13:28) which implied that no matter what we just told you, we have more news of why we can't possess the land like God has told us.

"Nevertheless, the people who live in the land are strong and the cities are fortified and very large…" The next word, "moreover," underscored their previous fears. "…moreover, we saw the descendants of Anak there, Amalek is living in the land and the Negev and the Hittites, and the Jebusites and the Amorrites ae living in the hill country, and the Canaanites are living by the sea and by the side of the Jordan." The bottom line is that "nevertheless" and "moreover" were code words for, "We *can't* do it", "Mission Impossible" in spite of the fact that "with God all things are possible." (Matthew 19:26)

They saw, they thought about it, they spoke it, and so they were.

> *"As a man thinketh in his heart so he is."*
> ~Pro-Verbs 23:7

> *"For there is no good tree which produces bad fruit, nor on the other hand, a bad tree which produces good fruit. For each tree is known by its own fruit. For men do not gather figs from thorns, nor do they pick grapes from a briar bush. The good man out of the good treasure of his heart brings forth what is good; and the evil man out of the evil treasure brings forth what is evil; for his mouth speaks from that which fills his heart."*
> ~Luke 6:43–45

The bottom line is that,

> *"…out of the abundance of the heart, the mouth speaks."*
> ~Luke 6:45

They were speaking what they couldn't do in spite of what God told them they could do.

This report, like all negative news, caused consternation among the people to the point that Caleb had to quite the people down before Moses. Then Caleb gave a positive report.

"...we should by ALL MEANS go up and TAKE POSSESION of it (the land that God gave them to possess). For WE SHALL OVERCOME (the land and the people)."
~Joshua 13:30, addition and emphasis mine

"BUT THE MEN who had gone up with him said, we ARE NOT ABLE TO GO UP AGAINST THE PEOPLE for they are TOO STRONG FOR US." So they gave out to the sons of Israel a BAD REPORT (a negative report) of the land which they had spied out, saying the land through which we have gone, in spying it out is a land that DEVOURS its inhabitants; and all the people whom we have saw in it are MEN OF GREAT SIZE."
~Numbers 13:31, addition and emphasis mine

How many times have you stepped out to peruse your desires, visions, dreams, and goals that God place within you and were stopped in your tracks by what others said, what others saw and used words like, "nevertheless" and "moreover."

God's Word says,

"I CAN DO all thing through Christ who strengthens me."
~Philippians 4:13, emphasis mine

The world says, "You *can't do...*"

There real reason that they could not do what God said they could do is because of their sight, their thinking, and what they confessed.

Job said the reason that all of the bad stuff happened was not God but himself. Job took 100% of the responsibility for his troubles on himself.

"For the thing which I greatly feared is come upon me, and that which I was afraid of is come unto me."

~Job 3:25

There is a natural law called The Law of Attraction which simply states that what you project out by your thoughts and your mouth will be attracted to you like a magnet. This is what the negative report projected out and came back to bite them.

"There also we saw the Nephilim (the sons of Anak are part of the Nephilim); and we (the mighty leaders of the tribes of Israel) BECAME LIKE GRASSHOPPERS in our OWN SIGHT, and so we WERE IN THEIR SIGHT."

~Numbers 13:33, addition and emphasis mine

Joshua and Caleb thought in their minds, *we can do it, by all means we should do it, and we should possess the land.* The cause and effect was that the others didn't, and they did. The lesson is that if you are going to become prosperous and successful biblically, then you are going to have to see differently, think differently, speak differently, and act differently.

CHAPTER FIVE

MANY WELLS/SPRINGS IN THE LAND

Too many times when something bad happens to us, we—or at least I—tend to give up. For example, you may lose your job and believe that your source of income has dried up, but the prosperous and successful individual will persevere and not give up but begin to unleash their Aggressive Faith. They realize that sometimes the "Weight-challenged lady sings."

Let me share a couple of my stories and then some principles from my life.

After graduating from school, I got my first job at a rehabilitation hospital. I stayed there for two years then accepted another job doing speech therapy in homes, hospitals, and prisons. One day at a team meeting, four people dressed in suits informed us that in thirty days they were shutting the company down. People were crying and cursing. I believe I saw a couple of people biblically *gnashing* their teeth. Some even asked me to go out drinking with them.

I did the best thing that I could ever do—I called Brenda, my wife. I told her what had just happened, and I heard these words, "Praise God, I wonder what He has for us next?"

A wave of peace that "surpasses all comprehension and understanding" (Philippians 4:6–7) came over me. What a woman. What a Pro-Verbs 31 woman! Look up Pro-Verbs 31 to read a description.

What happened next? I became the full-time Speech Pathologist of a hospital. I worked there for years, and then I was blessed with the opportunity to go to Africa.

I recently found a diary of my African adventure, and in it I had written down this story.

Back in 2005 I was blessed with a *free* trip to Africa, with the honor of teaching alongside a mentor, Baba (father) Bruce Coble, at a Youth with a Mission (Y.W.A.M.) Discipleship Training School (D.T.S.) in Kenya, Africa. That is another story for another time.

When I returned from Africa, back to my job as a Speech-Language Pathologist at a hospital, things were wonderful. For two weeks people were asking all kinds of questions and everyone wanted to see my pictures. I was even nominated by my boss for The Frist Humanitarian Award—a prestigious award within the hospital systems—and actually won. Life was good. I had a full time position, and I had full time benefits. I was living what I considered to be a blessed and abundant life. You could almost hear the birds sing along with Gordon McRae as he belted out the familiar song from the film version of the musical, *Oklahoma*, "Oh what a beautiful morning." I *did* have a wonderful feeling. Everything *was* going my way.

Suddenly, the songtrack shifted into a Bruce Cockburn song, "The Whole Night Sky," because it truly felt like a wind came out of nowhere and knocked me off my feet.

A couple of weeks after returning from my great adventure, *Ka-Boom!* The proverbial hammer fell. I was called into the boss's office where the Chief Financial Officer, the Human Resources Director, and my boss were waiting for me. I was informed that they were cutting my hours to part time, and I would lose benefits. The CFO told me, "It is nothing personal." Well, it was for me. Wow, talk about a sucker punch. As I stood there gasping for air, I could feel my flesh—my carnal nature—being activated. I was in shock. I watched as all of them except for my boss walked away. I went into my office in a fit of anger—I was in the flesh, the carnal nature—I began packing up my stuff in boxes, throwing things in right and left. My boss tried to calm me down, but I would have no part of it. I was throwing the largest pity party known to mankind.

I even took my Frist Humanitarian Award of the wall and asked my boss, "Do you know what this means?"

She said, No, what?

My response, "Absolutely nothing!"

After I cooled down I apologized to my boss and told her, "I may be a part time Speech Therapist, but I will do my job like I am a full time Speech Therapist."

And I did for a few more years. I ended up leaving after fifteen years of service. At one point my hospital and another hospital were going to split my time between the two so I could be full time, but the other hospital withdrew the offer, and I was back to being part time.

My friend, sonic partner, mentor, pastor, Sonic Sensei Wayne Berry came alongside me and spoke into my life. He told me there were many wells in the land. When one dries up there are more waters. This was based on Isaiah 12:3 and Psalm 84:5 and many other verses in the Word. Sure enough, "as sure as the sun rises"—a line from a Wayne Berry song—God met our *"needs according to His riches in glory in Christ Jesus,"* and their ain't no shortage in glory or Christ Jesus! (Philippians 4:13) I accepted those words by faith, shared them with my wife, Brenda, and we never missed a bill, a meal, or anything. We kept on being tithers and givers walking in the economy of the Lord versus the economy of the world.

In 2021, sixteen years later, we both are retired and starting a new adventure. Someone said, "We are glad that you did not retire, but re-fired." The heading on my Facebook page puts it this way:

I AM RETIRED REBOOTED REFRESHED REPRISTINATED REBORN RECON-FIGURED REFIRED REPENTED REJOICING RUMINATING!

Here is a look at part of that vision, and then I want to share you some prosperity and success principles as we live the abundant life (as we define it).

1. "When life hands you lemons, squeeze it and make lemonade." (W. Clement Stone) I have heard this saying for years but did not realize that it was a quote of a contemporary and friend of Napoleon Hill, a protégé of Andrew Carnegie and author of the influential motivational book, *Think and Grow Rich*. My lemon was being cut back to part time with minimal, if any, benefits. Brenda and I put the squeeze on by faith and were able to quench our thirst with sweet lemonade.

2. I was reading a book by Jack Canfield, co-author of *Chicken Soup for the Soul*, called *The Success Principles: How to Get from Where You Are to Where You Want to Be*. One of the principles was is "Become an Inverse Paranoid." Jack learned this principle from his mentor W. Clement Stone, the lemons to lemonade guy. Stone "chose to believe the world was plotting to do good. Instead of seeing every difficult or challenging event as a negative, he saw it for what it could be, something that was meant to enrich him, empower him, or advance his causes." I am thinking the proverbial using negative things as a stepping stone to the next level of advancement. It also said that if you take three steps forward and two steps back, you are still ahead one step.

3. I believe that many of the principles that successful people have used are Biblical Principles. *"And we know that all things (good, bad, and ugly) work together (synergistically) for good (and not bad) to those who love the Lord (me and you) and are called according to His purpose."*

Remember that one of the definitions of Success is accomplishing the purposes of God in our life. Jesus' purpose for coming to earth was "to destroy the works of the d-evil." (1 John 3:8) I believe that when Jesus became a curse on the tree/cross (Galatians 3:13–14) that the works of the d-evil to (1) steal our desires (2) kill our visions (3) destroy our dreams, that Jesus came and turned around the d-evil's purpose and gave us an Abundant Life. (John 10:10)

4. "God has many wells/springs in the land." (Wayne Berry) The two passages/verses that Wayne shared with me were Isaiah 12:3 and Psalm 84:5, but there are more in the Word.

> *"Therefore (see verse 2) you will joyously draw water from the springs of salvation (deliverance; hence aid, victory, prosperity: - deliverance, health, help (-ing), salvation, save, saving (health), welfare). And in that day you will say, give thanks to the Lord, call on His name. Make known His deeds among the peoples; make them remember that His name is exalted. Praise the Lord in song, for He has done excellent things; let this be made known throughout the earth."*
>
> ~Isaiah 12:3–5, AMP, additions and emphasis mine

*"How blessed (supremely happy so as to be envied and spiritu-
ally prosperous with life-joy and satisfaction in God's favor and
salvation (rescue or safety (physically or morally): - deliver, health,
salvation, save, saving), regardless of their outward conditions) is
the man whose strength is in "You" in whose heart are the highways
to Zion (set on pilgrimage). Passing (not setting up camp in the
valley) through the valley of Baca (tears/weeping) they make it
a spring; the early rain also covers it with blessings. They go from
strength to strength, every one of them appears before God in Zion
(you are not alone in the journey)."*
　　　　　~Psalm 84:5–7, AMP, additions and emphasis mine

Wayne also sent me this reminder: "Keep in mind that some of
those wells can overflow." When one well dries up there are others
in the land.

This reminds me of the MSI principle—Multiple Sources of
Income. I was listening to positive thinker and motivational speaker,
Bob Proctor, telling us to never rely on one source of income. If that
one source dries up, you will not have any money coming in. He
told us to always have Multiple Sources of Income, so when one
dries up, the others keep on flowing.

In my new season of Rodney Lewis Boyd my multiple sources
of income are Bible Teacher, Motivational Speaker, Author, Speech
Pathologist, Musician, Worship Leader, Martial Artist, Consultant,
Mentor, and Disciple Maker. And not only that, but part of my MSI
system includes my social security, the IRS refunds, 401K, investments, the Lord moving on hearts to give, etc. All of my MSIs comes
from the headwaters of God Himself who is my supply.

*"And my God will liberally supply (fill to the full) your every need
according to His riches in glory in Christ Jesus."*
　　　　　　　　　　　　　　　~Philippians 4:19, AMP

No, I don't believe that manna will fall from heaven or quail will
come or a raven will bring bread—all the ways God met men's
needs back in the day. I am open to all of that, but I believe that

God typically uses humans in various forms of meeting my needs. I will get up in the morning with an expectancy from God to meet our needs, and I will do like Evelyn Roberts, Oral Robert's darling wife, and check the mailbox to see if the blessing came yet.

"Give (me doing the giving), and [gifts] will be given (back) to you (Rodney Lewis Boyd): good measure, pressed down, shaken together, and running over will they (men) pour into [the pouch formed by] the bosom [of your robe and used as a bag]. For with the measure you deal out/give/sow [with the measure you use when you confer benefits on others], it WILL BE (not might be) be measured back to you."
~Luke 6:38, additions and emphasis mine

"Do not be deceived (don't fool yourself), God is not mocked; for whatever (good, bad or ugly) a man sows, this he will also reap."
~Galatians 3:5, additions and emphasis mine

"Do not be deceived and deluded and misled; god will not allow Himself to be sneered at (scorned, disdained, or mocked by mere pretensions or professions, or by His precepts being set aside). He inevitably deludes himself who attempts to delude God.] For WHATEVER (no limit) a man sows, that and that only is what he will reap."
~Galatians 6:7, AMP, additions and emphasis mine

NOTE: The principle of sowing and reaping in the natural is that a seed will go into the soil and produce in like kind. The soil is no respecter of the seed or the one sowing. It will work for religious people with traditions, it will work for followers of Jesus, it will work for non-Christians, heathens, pagans, agnostics, and atheist alike. If someone sows corn, corn will produce; if someone sows poison ivy, poisons ivy will produce.

"For he who sows to his own flesh (lower, carnal nature, sensuality)

will from the flesh reap decay and ruin and destruction, but he who sows to the Spirit will from the spirit reap eternal life."
~Galatians 6:8, AMP, additions and emphasis mine

CHAPTER SIX

HOLD YOUR HEAD UP

Since my sabbatical, I have been reenergized in every area of my life. One area is teaching the Word of God and teaching motivational messages—it is hard for me to separate the two. Here is one that speaks to me, hopefully it will speak to you also.

> *To experience true Biblical Prosperity and Success you can't be constantly looking down.*

One of my favorite songs of encouragement is by a group called Argent. The song is "Hold Your Head Up."

The gist of the song is that things can be bad, but be encouraged and don't allow the bad to get you down. Instead, realize that you can take it. When people see you moving on and people start staring at you, let them stare and burn their eyes. They will even shout at you but, don't let it change what you are doing.

So, what should you do? Keep holding your head up.

The other day, I was recovering from a sore back. I was not able to walk very well. Brenda was down in the den, and I was up in the next level of the house. I asked Brenda to watch me walk to compare how I was walking since I hurt my back. I felt like I was walking better, so I turned around and began to walk. The first thing she said was not about how good I was walking. Instead, she said, "You need to hold your head up, you're looking down at the ground."

She was right. I noticed since the stroke that I am always looking down to the ground. I guess since I had fallen multiple times before *the* stroke—I never say *my* stroke since Jesus bore it on the cross—and during the stroke I have fallen, it developed me into being extra careful when walking up and down stairs or just walking in general so I would not fall again. I knew this principle well.

The other day, I was talking to a young man in my office who is a friend of mine. As I was talking, he was looking down to the ground—something he does often. I called his name and told him to hold his head up and look me in the eyes, which he did with a sheepish grin. Brenda's words came back to me: "You need to hold your head up."

At Bill Taylor's Bushido School of Karate, whenever we pass out belts after an exam, Sensei Bill Taylor walks down the line, shaking their hands. More than once I have heard Sensei tell them:

1. Shake my hand with a good grip, it shows confidence.
2. Hold your heads up and look me in the eyes. Then he tells them (the kids) to go and find the one who brought them here to take karate (usually parents or grandparents) and to give them your old belt and hug them and tell them thank you. This is the "attitude of gratitude" that is just a couple of the lessons learned in the dojo.

Another lesson I learned in the dojo (practice floor) is that when you are going up and down the floor throwing a technique, "hold your head up." The principle is that where your gaze goes so goes your technique. If you are in a fight, you need to keep your head up and your eyes focused on where you want you technique to go—whether you are in a street fight or sparring. You need to keep your head up and your chin down and your hands up. An additional thing to remember, where your knee points is where your kick will go. The principle of "hold you head up" applies to every area in your life. Too many people, myself included, look down, dejected, defeated before they even start. I believe that if we keep our heads up, keep our *zanshin* awareness of our surroundings, and be aggressively controlled in our self-defense, then we will succeed. Before you can physically hold your head up, you must hold your head up in your mind.

CHAPTER SEVEN

BLACK BELT VIRTUES
PARADIGM FOR PROSPERITY AND SUCCESS

A paradigm is the way we think, speak, and act about anything. I believe that many of the principles I learned in karate shaped my paradigm—the way I thought, spoke, and acted—on my Black Belt journey.

Way back in the early '70s I began to study the martial arts in Wado Ryu Karate—the way of harmony and peace with the empty hand. At the time I was 19 years old, and today I celebrated my 70th birthday. The full story of my karate journey is found in my book *Never Run A Dead Kata: Lessons I Learned in the Dojo*.

I am convinced that the many of the principles and lessons I learned in my study of karate are also effective for success in life and business.

In the official Student Guide there is a section called Black Belt Virtues, which reads:

As a dedicated student of the Martial Arts, I will live by the principles of the Black Belt.

MODESTY

COURTESY

INTEGRITY

SELF-CONTROL

PERSEVERANCE

INDOMINTABLE SPIRIT

There is no doubt that these virtues will help guarantee success in karate and in every endeavor in our lives. Success merely means to accomplish the purposes set before us. Earl Nightingale, famous for personal development, defines success as, "the progressive realization of a worthy ideal." Here are some definitions that not only define the words but define us. In this section we will give a definition of the word from the dictionary and then the definition found in the Student Guide handbook from Bushido School of Karate.

MODESTY: (1) the quality of being modest; freedom from vanity, boastfulness, etc. (2) regard for decency of behavior, speech, dress, etc. (3) simplicity; moderation.

Being humble and not bragging.

COURTESY: (1) excellence of manners or social conduct; polite behavior (2) a courteous, respectful, or considerate act or expression. (3) Indulgence, consent, or acquiescence: (4) Favor, help, or generosity

Being kind and respectful to others.

INTEGRITY: (1) adherence to moral and ethical principles; soundness of moral character; honesty (2) the state of being whole, entire, or undiminished (3) to preserve the integrity of the empire (4) a sound, unimpaired, or perfect condition

Being honest and true to your word.

SELF-CONTROL: control or restraint of oneself or one's actions, feelings

Being in control of your actions, emotions, and thoughts.

PERSEVERANCE: steady persistence in a course of action, a purpose, a state, etc., especially in spite of difficulties, obstacles, or discouragement.

To stick with something no matter what obstacles have to be overcome.

INDOMINTABLE SPIRIT: that cannot be subdued or overcome, as persons, will, or courage; unconquerable

The human spirit that can never be broken.

As we are faced with various obstacles designed to stop us in our tracks and never accomplishing our goals, the Black Belt Virtues are invaluable in our quest for success.

As I worked out in the dojo for many years, sweating, there was a sign on the dojo wall that I would see throughout the workout sessions that read, "The only time that sweat comes before success is in the dictionary." It is true in the karate world, it is true in the natural world, and it is true in the spiritual world.

CHAPTER EIGHT

BALL OF CONFUSION

NOTE: This is an explanation of why there is negative and positive in this world. It seems like this Ball Of Confusion (Planet Earth) has been going on since the fall of man and continues on to this very day with no hope in sight of resolution. Everyone has their own theory, so why shouldn't I throw my theory in the ring?

NOTE TO THE NOTE: Some may wonder if I am mixing in new age mumbo jumbo into my faith. The answer is an emphatic *no way*. I am convinced that many of the positive teachers, many new age teachers, and many religious teachers confiscated the teachings and principles of God.

> *"The Bible is not new age but old age that the new age has stolen."*
> ~Rodfucious

According to National Geographic, "Earth, our home planet, is a world unlike any other. The third planet from the sun, Earth is the only place in the known universe confirmed to host life. With a radius of 3,959 miles, Earth is the fifth largest planet in our solar system, and it's the only one known for sure to have liquid water on its surface."

Earth, mother earth, the blue planet, the third planet, the third rock from the sun are all names for the Mother Ship called Earth—aka The Ball of Confusion. Out of the nine planets in the known solar system—eight if you don't count Pluto—Earth is the one planet we know about that is inhabited with human beings. Larry Norman, one of the originators of Christian Rock and Roll, had a song called

"U.F.O." that claims if there was life on other planets, God would have already made provision for the salvation of their inhabitants. According to various sources, as of 2021 there are 7.9 billion people currently living on Earth, not counting all of the dead people of the past.

I don't know how many people have ever existed or will exist. But one thing that I do know:

"For God so loved the world—7.9+ billion people, past, present and future inhabitants—that He (Father God) gave His only begotten Son (Jesus) that (the reason for the giving) whosoever (open to the 7.9 + billion people) believes (trusts in, clings to, relies on, adheres to, relies on) in Him (Jesus) should not perish (die separated from God) BUT (in contrast to dying separated from God) have ever-lasting (lasting forever) life (not death, and that more abundantly, aka abundant life)."

~John 3:16 emphasis and additions mine Ruminator Style,

At the time of this writing, we are currently living in what I call, *"a world wide pandemic of fear* fueled by *systemic sin* manifested by *systemic hate* with *systemic roots of bitterness* with a stranglehold on the minds and hearts of humankind."

According to the wise preacher, Solomon,

"That which has been is that which will be, and that which has been done is that which will be done. So there is nothing new under the sun."

~Ecclesiastes 1:9–10

Ever since the fall of man in the Garden (Genesis 3:1–24), there has been trouble, death and dying. In the first family unit—man, woman, children—the roots of sin from the garden has grown into envy, hate, religious disputes, and murder. (Genesis 4:1–16) The problem has exacerbated from then until now. History is wroth with a constant thread of wars and rumors of wars, vain attempts to live in peace with multiple peace treaties which really are nothing but documents of domination from one side over the other.

The more I ruminate on the problems of the world and the lack of a solution to Pandemic Systemic Sin, the more I find myself ruminating on the Kingdom of God versus the kingdom of darkness—ruled by the god of this world, satan.

There are two realms (Kingdoms, Matthew 6:33, Matthew 6:9) that are at odds with each other. One realm is Heaven (where God is King) and Earth (where the d-evil is known as the *god of this world* and *the prince of the power of the air*, 2 Corinthians 4:4, Ephesians 2:2–4).

I believe there is a misconception about God and His rule on Planet Earth. The old song declares, "He's got the whole world in His hands…He's got the whole, wide, world in His hands." It is a great song. I have sung it. I will sing it again because in my mind, He is God and while the world looks out of control, I know that nothing has surprised God, and in the end, He triumphs!

Theologians have pronounced that the nature of God is this:

1. God in Omnipotent =God is all-powerful
2. God is Omniscience = God is all-knowing
3. God is Omnipresent = God is everywhere at the same time.

When you roll the three characteristics of the One God—not a polytheistic view of God—you have what is known as the sovereignty of God.

NOTE: The words Omnipotent, Omniscience and Omnipresent are not found in the Scriptures.

SOVEREIGNTY: (1) supreme power or authority (2) the authority of a state to govern itself or another state (3) a self-governing state. Now, this is a political definition for Kingdoms and governments.

SOVEREIGN/POTENTATE: dunastēs (doo-nas'-tace)=From G1410; a ruler or officer: - of great authority, mighty, potentate. G1410: dunamai (doo'-nam-ahee)=Of uncertain affinity; to be able or possible: - be able, can (do, + -not), could, may, might, be possible, be of power.

NOTE: In Strong's concordance, the word sovereign is not found in the Word but potentate is found one time in I Timothy 6:15)

The question is, is God sovereign? According to the Word of God, yes.

> *"I charge you in the presence of God, who gives life to all things, and of Christ Jesus, who testified the good confession before Pontius Pilate, that you keep the commandment without stain or reproach until the appearing of our Lord Jesus Christ, which He will bring about at the proper time—He who is blessed and only Sovereign (Potentate), the King of kings and the Lord of lords, who alone possesses immortality and dwells in approachable light or can see. To Him be honor and eternal dominion! Amen."*
> ~I Timothy 6:13–16, addition mine

NOTE: IF God is Omnipotent, Omniscient, Omnipresent, and Sovereign in the sense of what theologians say, and His will is what we see here on Planet Earth, then I have a problem—*not* with God, but with theologians and denominations that just accept the evil, negative, chaos and pandemic of fear. I believe and know that God is the last authority in the world, but I also believe and know that there is something more than meets the eye. I believe what that is, is revealed in the Lord's Prayer. (Matthew 6:9–15, Luke 11:1–4) I could be wrong, but I think I'm right.

The boys (aka the disciples) apparently had been watching John's (the Dipper/Baptist) pray. They came to Jesus and requested:

> *"Lord, teach us to pray* just as *John also taught his disciples."*
> ~Luke 11:1, emphasis mine

NOTE: This is odd to me. The one who they were following was once again praying:

> *"…Jesus was praying in a certain place (what's your certain place), after He finished (there is a start, middle and finishing to prayer)…"*
> ~Luke 11:1, additions and emphasis mine

I noticed that Jesus did not get upset that they were watching John and his disciples and wanted Jesus to be like John. No, He merely began to teach them *Kingdom Prayers.*

NOTE: I am not going to do a total teaching on The Lord's Prayer. I want to focus on the Heaven and Earth aspect of this prayer for God's Kingdom will (wish and desire) to be manifested.

- YOUR KINGDOM COME

KINGDOM: basileia (bas-il-i'-ah)=From G935; properly royalty, that is, (abstractly) rule, or (concretely) a realm (literally or figuratively): - kingdom, + reign. G935: basileus (bas-il-yooce') =Probably from G939 (through the notion of a foundation of power); a sovereign (abstractly, relatively or figuratively): - king. G939: basis (bas'-ece)=From βαίνω bainō (to walk); a pace ("base"), that is, (by implication) the foot: - foot.

1. Extrapolated Kingdom Definition
2. Royalty
3. Rule
4. Realm (literally and figuratively)
5. Kingdom + Reign
6. A Foundation of Power
7. Sovereign
8. A walk, a pace
9. Foot

> *"The KINGDOM OF GOD is not meat or drink but (1) Righteousness= equity the quality of being fair or impartial, something that is fair and just (2) Peace= prosperity: - one, peace, quietness, rest, + set at one again. (3) Joy= cheerfulness, that is, calm delight: - gladness IN THE HOLY GHOST."*
> ~Romans 14:17, addition and emphasis mine

> *"Seek (keep on diligently seek) first the KINGDOM OF GOD and (in addition to) His RIGHTEOUSNESS (equity the quality of being fair or impartial, something that is fair and just) and all*

of these THINGS (food, drink, clothing) will be added to you."
~Matthew 6:33, addition and emphasis mine

NOTE: We are called to be Kingdom Seekers and Christ Followers. I always like to read Matthew 6:33, like this, "Seek first the KINGDOM OF GOD (not the kingdom of Rod)."

NOTE: When we are praying for His Kingdom to *come*, the implication is that this Kingdom is somewhere else other than here. We are praying that the royalty, rule, realm, reign, foundation of power (exousia=delegated authority, duNAMis=dynamic, miraculous, ability) to come from headquarters (heaven) to the outpost (where we are envoys).

- YOUR WILL BE DONE

NOTE: I will start off this next section with a quote from Bob Mumford's book *The King And You* about the word, will.

"The Kingdom is a condition in the heart of the believer where the will of God is done, even as it is in heaven."
~Bob Mumford

"We need to understand that there are two different words used in the Greek for our English word will, as it is used throughout Scriptures. One is boulema, the other is thelema. Boulema, means the eternal counsels of God which are unfolding through the ages—His purpose, His determination. It is going to be done whether you and I like it or not. God's intention will come to pass. However thelema, which means God's wish or desire, most often depends upon the response of each individual for fulfillment."
~Bob Mumford

"Referring again to Jesus' words in Matthew 6:10, "Thy kingdom come, thy will be done in earth as it is in heaven", do you see this prayer brings the wish or desire of God into an EARTHLY SETTING? Without getting theological or complicated, could you

understand when I say God's will (His wish, desire) IS NOT being done on earth as it is in heaven? This has nothing to do with the eternal counsels of the Almighty, but rather His intimate intervention in the affairs of our lives."

~Bob Mumford

"It IS NOT the will (wish, desire) of God that divorce, family problems, poverty, sickness, continue in this world UNCHALLENGED."
~Bob Mumford

NOTE: I highly recommend Bob Mumford's book *The King And You.*

It is God's will that we are inviting into our world the Kingdom and demonstrating by our actions of faith, Kingdom Living. Some theologians, religious people, and denominations believe that whatever happens to us is the will of a sovereign God, so why resist and struggle? Just lay back and accept the will of God, learn your lessons, and be matured. After all He is sovereign. My thought process is *if* it is the will of God for you to be sick, dis-eased, dis-comforted, and dys-functional, *then* never go to the doctor, never take medicine, never go to the hospital, never have surgery. Just stay sick and accept the will of God. No, I believe that we innately know that something is wrong, and we will do everything we can to make it right.

Remember, there are two places—earth and heaven. I look up to heaven, and I do not see poverty, sin, sickness, dis-ease, dis-comfort, dis-stress, dys-function, hate, wars, riots, fear, racism—fill in the blank of negative thing that you see on planet earth. I look up to heaven, and I see forgiveness, healing, ease, comfort, no stress, functionality, love, peace, no riots, faith and not fear, all colors of people in harmony. *If* you are going to pray for "Thy Kingdom come" and "Thy will (wish, desire) be done (manifested)" then you better be believing for the positive and not the negative.

"Thy (our heavenly Father) Kingdom (rule, reign, foundation of power) Thy (our heavenly Father) will (wish, desire) be done (manifested and accomplished) on earth (where the d-evil is the god

of this world and the prince of the power of the air, where there is the cursed planet and people, total negativity, dis-ease, dis-comfort, dis-stress, dys-function) AS IT IS (the model of what is wanted on earth) in heaven (where there is the Sovereign God, with blessing, total positivity, ease, comfort, stress, function)."

~Matthew 6:10, Ruminator Style

NOTE: Why pray to God for what you already have here on earth? Pray heaven down to earth. I remember singing that song, "Heaven came *Down* and glory filled my soul."

- ## THE PRINCIPLES (LAWS) OF VIBRATION AND FREQUENCY

I believe that there are many laws of the universe that the Creator of the Universe set into motion when He spoke into existence His thoughts, and they became reality. The principle/law of gravity is a fact. As it works, if Billy Graham and Adolph Hitler jump off of the Empire State Building, both will be pulled down to the concrete sidewalks of New York City, looking like toppings on a New York Style pizza. When you violate the Law of Gravity the cause and effect will be like tipping over dominos. (See what I did there? Pizza/Dominos?) The same Law of Gravity keeps us from flying off of planet Earth into the sun and burning up (Crispy Critters).

There are multiple natural laws in effect that affects us. How we utilize these laws determines if our lives are positive or negative.

"As a man thinketh in his heart so he is."

~Pro-Verbs 23:7

"…out of the abundance of the heart a man speaks."

~Luke 6:45

I believe that all throughout the Word of God, God's principles are laid out for us to live by, and the violation of the principles will bring consequences.

NOTE: Many people who believe and teach these principles do not acknowledge that they are God-given. They tend to believe that *they* are the ones in control based on their own volition (free will) that God has given us, to choose.

These principles/laws are based in science—man's understanding of empirical evidence.

One of my favorite natural laws is The Law of Vibration.

NOTE: I don't understand a lot of the principles that we live with every day. Some may be able to explain them and even understand them to a point, but not me.

I don't understand how electricity works, but that does not stop me from turning on the lights and enjoying being able to see. I don't understand the physiological principles of respiration, but that does not stop me from inhaling the good air and experiencing the transference of oxygen to the blood and then exhaling out bad air. I don't understand the principles of the internet—which can be used for good, bad, and ugly purposes—but that does not stop me from logging in and searching the World Wide Web. You get the idea.

According to the scientists, the world is made up of vibrations and frequencies. Everything has a frequency that determines what you see and experience here on planet Earth. For example, take your hand and knock a desk or table. It is solid. Hit it as hard as you can (be careful not to break your hand). Now, go dive into a swimming pool or river. The fluid nature of the water is good for drinking, bathing, swimming, etc. Both are made up of vibrations, vibrating at a different frequency at a molecular level. Imaging diving into a pool filled with water that is vibrating at the same frequency of a desk or table.

Bam!

As a 2nd Degree Black Belt in karate, I have never broken a brick or a board, but I know people who have. The molecular vibrating makeup of a brick or wood makes the objects harder than my fleshly hand. There is nothing worse than attempting to break a brick or board but breaking the bones in your hand instead.

As a Speech-Language Pathologist who happens to be a follower of the Anointed One, Christ Jesus, who is anointed with yoke-breaking, burden-lifting, oppression-removing, healing power of the Holy Ghost, I have worked for 31 years with Speech Development and the disruptions of the speech patterns including voice orders and disorders. I have utilized an instrument called the Visi Pitch. When I am working with a patient with voice dis-orders, I have them speak into a microphone that will translate into vibrations and frequencies on a monitor. There are frequencies for certain sounds that we can match to retrain voice frequencies. The therapy is to have the patient visually see the vibrations/frequencies of a normal pattern and then have them match those patterns with their patterns of vibrations/frequencies of speech. The concept is that over a period of time with repetition of correct vibrations and frequency their brain patterns will be shifted, and their voice will improve. That is called neuroplasticity.

The process of speaking and hearing are made up of vibrations and frequency. When we inhale, oxygen goes through our nose and mouth and travels to the level of the vocal folds, aka vocal cords, that draws the vocal folds together—much like when you are standing in a hot shower and the shower curtain is drawn to your legs, aka the Bernoulli's Law/Principle/Effect. When you exhale, the breath breaks open the vocal folds which start vibrating at a certain frequency and travel out through the resonating cavities.

The frequency of vocal folds plus resonating cavities= why you sound the way you do.

These vibrations leave the mouth in the form of words, and another human receives that vibrations by their ears (auricle or pinna, what you see on the side of the head), and then the vibrations travel down the ear canal striking the tympanic membrane (aka the ear drum). The vibration/frequency is turned into mechanical energy where three bones set into motion hydraulic energy in the inner ear at the location of the cochlea (a snail like shell) that has fluid and tiny hair cells (tuned to certain frequencies) that snap and send electrical energy through the VIIIth Cranial Nerve (aka the Acoustic Nerve) to the Brain (Control Central) where the vibrations/frequencies are decoded into understandable words and then encoded and sent back to the receiver.

So you have a system of transmitters/receivers that communicate via vibrations and frequencies. All I can say at this juncture is:

"I will praise thee; for I am fearfully and wonderfully made: marvelous are thy works; and that my soul knoweth right well."

~Psalm 139:14

"I will give thanks and praise to You, for I am fearfully and wonderfully made; Wonderful are Your works, and my soul knows it very well."

~Psalm 139:14 AMP

Here are a couple of more examples of vibration and frequency.

1. Guitar sounds. Each string of the guitar is tuned to difference frequencies. If you look at an electric tuner you can see the frequency/vibration for each string. E, A, D, G, B, E all are tuned, and when you finger the certain chords different sounds emit. When played with other instruments you can create great harmonies. If a string is out of tune or a chord is played wrong, you will be out of harmony or create dissonance (lack of harmony among musical notes, a tension or clash resulting from the combination of two disharmonious or unsuitable elements). It is like the earth vibration/frequency and heaven vibration/frequency, there is negative dissonance. It is like "on negative dissonance as it is in positive harmony." I recently saw a video of my guitar hero, Phil Keaggy, placing a camera in the sound hole of his guitar and play a song, and you could see the vibration patterns of his strings that were tuned to the certain frequencies that strings vibrate. Amazing.

2. The Kingdom of God (John 3:1–8). Jesus is explaining the concept of being born again, born anew, born from above to Nicodemus (Nick at Night) a religious leader. I believe that Jesus is speaking of being born to a new frequency and vibration—but that's just me. During the explanation Nick has questions. They are logical questions but cannot be understood

by logic. Jesus response was, "That which is bornof the flesh is flesh (the natural) and that which is born of the Spirit (Holy) is spirit (human, the innermost man, the lamp of the Lord, the Supernatural). The further explanation resounds with what we are talking about. "The wind blows where it wishes and you hear the sound (vibration) of it, (Him) but do not know where it comes from (can't rely on the senses) and is going; so is everyone who is born of the Spirit." Nicks response much like the thing we can't see or explain, "How can these things be?" (John 3:6–9)

- WHAT DOES THIS HAVE TO DO WITH "ON EARTH AS IT IS IN HEAVEN"?

In my mind, everything.

When God first thought (in His imagination) about creating, He spoke into existence *Heaven* And *Earth*.

> *"In the beginning God created (1) heavens (2) earth."*
> ~Genesis 1:1, addition mine

At this point it is talking about the heavens above us and the earth below us. The heavens (skies) are mandated from Heaven (headquarters).

The condition of this Creation is underscored throughout Genesis 1 with "and it was good" and even:

> *"God saw all that he had made, and behold, it was very good...."*
> ~Genesis 1:31

This included man.

> *"Then God said, Let Us (I am convinced that "Us"=the Father, Son, Holy Ghost) make man in Our (Father, Son, Holy Ghost) image (the Blueprint of the Spiritual DNA)."*
> ~Genesis 1:26, addition mine

"God created man in His own image (the Blueprint of the Spiritual DNA), in the image (the Blueprint of the Spiritual DNA), he (God) created him; male and female He created them (plural)."
~Genesis 1:27, addition mine

"God blessed them (plural) and God said to them (plural), be fruitful and multiply, and fill the earth and subdue it, and rule over the fish of the sky and over every living thing that moves (creeps) over the earth. Then God said, behold, I have given you every plant yielding seed that is on the surface (face) of all the earth, and every tree (including the tree of the knowledge of good and evil) which has fruit yielding seed; it shall be food for you; and to every beast of the earth and to every bird of the sky and to everything that moves (creeps) on the earth which has life, I have given every green plant for food..."
~Genesis 1:28–31, addition mine

This was the nature of planet earth. There was no negativity, no bad vibrations, and no skewed frequencies. This was what is known as God's *ultimate intention*.

This new world came with a warning label for A & E (aka Adam & Eve, man and wo-man, husband and wife, mankind).

"The Lord God commanded the man (Adam, Eve was not created yet) saying, "from any tree of the garden you may eat FREELY; but from the tree of the knowledge of good and evil you shall NOT eat from it, for in that day that you eat from it you shall surely die."
~Genesis 2:16–17, addition and emphasis mine

So, what happen, how did we get from there to now?

- HIGH TREASON VIA DISOBEDIENCE (Enter the dragon/serpent/d-evil)

Back in the Garden, the original state of Earth, we see the beginning of the end as we know it currently. Things were going well until the creep crept in. (Genesis 1:28, 30)

"Now the serpent (the creeping creep) was more crafty than any beast of the field which the Lord God had made (yes, satan is a created being and not God). And he (the creep) said to the woman, (one who had authority and dominion over the creep, as did Adam), "Indeed, has God said, you shall not eat from any tree of the garden?"
~Genesis 3:1, addition mine

The #1 temptation is to place doubt in God's Word. He did it with A & E, Jesus, and every believer in the Death, Burial, and Resurrection.

The woman responded and began carrying on a conversation with the d-evil.

NOTE: You don't have to have a conversation with him, just speak the Word, and "Be gone." I once heard Oral Roberts teach that the word *rebuke* means, "Stop it, that's enough!"

"The woman said to the serpent, from the fruit of the trees of the garden we may eat (actually not all of the trees), but from the fruit of the tree which is in the middle of the garden, God has said you shall not eat from it or touch it (actually God did not say anything about touching it), or you will die."
~Genesis 1:2–3, addition mine

Well, she got it mostly right, although to eat it you would have to touch it, so maybe technically she was correct.

The serpent started phase two by putting into the mind of woman about what God said and that He did not really mean it.

"The serpent said to the woman, you shall surely not die!"

NOTE: The d-evil counters God's good, positive Word with his bad and negative word. Then he plants in the thought that God is holding out on her.

"For God knows that in the day you eat from it your eyes will be opened, and you will be like God, knowing good and evil."
~Genesis 1:5

"When the woman saw that the tree (of the knowledge of good and evil) was good for food, and that it was a delight to the eyes, and that the tree was desirable to make one wise, she took from its fruit and ate; and she gave also *to her husband (Adam)* who was with her *and he ate."*
~Genesis 1:6, addition and emphasis mine

NOTE: Remember that God gave both the man and woman dominion (Genesis 1:26–30) even though the orders were to man, the man obviously told the woman because she knew what God had said. Another interesting thing, some think that the woman was all alone when the serpent crept into the Garden. But no, the man, the husband, Adam was right there as she "gave also to her husband *with her and he ate."* (Genesis 1:6) So, the head of the house should have stepped in and dealt with the d-evil. Instead he just stood by and allowed the creep to have his way with the woman.

The trifecta of temptation is complete, (1) The lust of the flesh (2) the lust of the eyes (3) the boastful pride of life. (1 John 2:16)

The cause and effect of succumbing to temptation was death. However, they did not just drop over dead. "...*for in the day that you eat from it you* shall surely die." (Genesis 2:17, emphasis mine) Well, they *did not die,* but I am convinced from that point death entered into their lives via the curse. They experienced separation of fellowship from God, pain entered in, sweat entered in, and after that for thousands of years people died physical and spiritually.

"Therefore, just as through one man (male, female, Adam, Eve) entered into the world and death through sin, and so death spread to all men, because all sinned."
~Romans 5:12, addition mine

There was a shift and change in the world that God created (a positive vibration) into a (negative vibration) that we see and experience today.

Adam and Eve committed high treason through disobedience and gave up their rights to rule and have dominion over to the serpent/d-evil, the "god of this world" of negativity.

• RESTORATION TO THE ULTIMATE INTENTION

God created Adam and Eve in Their (Father, Son, Holy Ghost) own image, and then He blessed them both and commissioned them with a mission. When they committed high treason by disobedience, on the surface it looked like God's Original Intention was thwarted by Original Sin. For a few thousand years God provided a way to connect with Him through sacrificial means (the blood of animals) via the tabernacles/temples. It was not a permanent solution, but help was on its way. The help came via a young, virgin girl who in obedience gave birth to the Messiah, the Christ.

• IN THE BEGINNING

-God created
-Man/Woman created in God's (Father, Son, Holy Spirit) own image and likeness
-God's likeness/image = The Blueprint/DNA passed on to Mankind
-Both man/woman were Blessed, Given Authority and Commissioned to reproduce

• THE FALL

-Adam and Eve committed High Treason via disobedience to the Word of God
-The Fallout of the Fall was Death (a physical separation from fellowship with God)
-The Fallout of the Fall opened the door to the curse/sickness/hardships/ physical THE CURSE

• RESTORATION

-Jesus (God in the flesh) came to earth via a young virgin girl as the Messiah/Christ/Savior
-Jesus lived for thirty years and then was baptized by the Father with the Holy Spirit

-Jesus went about under the Anointing of the Holy Spirit, doing good, removing oppression , healing for three years

-Jesus' purpose for coming to earth was to destroy the works of the d-evil, demonstrating the -Kingdom will of God on earth as it was in heaven.

- MISSION CONTINUES

-At the point of restoration is the Cross

-For God so loved the world that He gave His only begotten Son

-People had to believe in the Death, Burial, Resurrection of the Cross

-The cause and effect of the believing was restoration and deliverance from perishing.

-The problem is people don't understand that what happened "in the beginning" did not end

-Many Christians stay at the cross and never grow, never carry out the original intention.

-The Mission = Doing the same things (works Jesus did for three years) that Jesus did, even, greater

- THE RETURN

-At some point Jesus is going to return to collect the dead in Christ first then the rest of us

-This is the great snatching away of the saints called the Rapture to rescue us from the negative, systemic vibration and frequency of the d-evil.

- ON EARTH AS IT IS IN HEAVEN

We have talked before of how, when created, this world and everything in it was set into vibration with various frequencies. Before the fall the earth was in harmony with God's vibration and frequency. At the temptation man/woman chose to go to another vibration set into motion by the d-evil/the serpent. When Adam and Eve gave over to temptation they gave over to the d-evil the authority that God gave them, and the negative vibration took over planet earth. When Jesus came to the earth and demonstrate the Kingdom will of God with God's original vibration, miracles happened.

I believe that under the rule of the god of this world, the prince of the power of the air along with the course (the way the world works) the negative vibration and frequency is in play. This is why there is so much evil and bad thing happening to good and bad people. It is why all around the world there is a *Pandemic Of Fear* (not faith) fueled by *Systemic Sin* (disobedience) manifested by *Systemic Hate* (not love) with people's minds squeezed by the *Systemic Roots Of Bitterness.*

The only hope (confident expectation) is that the followers of Jesus will come and bring the *Vibration/Frequency Of Heaven* to *The Vibration/Frequency Of The D-Evil) On Earth.* The *Vibration Of Sin* must be dealt with by the *Vibration Of The Cross.*

I believe that Jesus taught us how to pray against the d-evil vibration when He taught them to pray

> *"Thy (The Fathers) Kingdom (rule, reign, foundation of power) come (from heaven), Thy will (wish, desire) be done (accomplished and manifested) on earth (where there is the d-evil's negative frequency and vibration) AS IT IS (where the positive vibration/ frequency DNA, BLUEPRINT is) in heaven (forgiveness, deliverance, healing, peace, joy, righteousness, ease, comfort, love, function, no stress, etc. "*
>
> ~Matthew 6:10, addition and emphasis mine

CHAPTER NINE

THE ORIGINAL PARADIGM
IN THE BEGINNING

I believe that you can never have Biblical Success and Prosperity unless you have a paradigm shift. The original paradigm created by God was very good. It was not until the sin of disobedience when Adam and Eve committed high treason that the paradigms shifted towards the negative. In the next few chapters we will see how the cursed paradigm—as the result of a curse of eating forbidden fruit from a tree—was reversed by another tree—the cross.

I believe the secret to success and prosperity lies on the other side of the tree (cross) with the death, burial and resurrection of Jesus. We have looked at the initial creation, but now we look at creation in view of paradigms.

PARADIGM: (1) a set of forms all of which contain a particular element, especially the set of all inflected forms based on a single stem or theme. (2) A display in fixed arrangement of such a set, as boy's, boys, boys, boys'. (3) An example serving as a model; pattern. (4) A framework containing the basic assumptions, ways of thinking, and methodology that are commonly accepted by members of a scientific community (5) such a cognitive framework shared by members of any discipline or group.

~Dictionary.com

PARADIGM: "Paradigms are a multitude of habits that guide every move you make. They affect the way you eat, the way you walk, even the way you talk. They govern your communication, your work habits, your successes and your failures."

~Bob Proctor

This concept of a paradigm is fascinating to me. To some it is some new age enlightenment of mumbo-jumbo (I have used this term before), some P.M.A. (Positive Mental Attitude) taught by charlatans trying to get your money by making you think that you can *Think and Grow Rich*—the name of a wonderful book by Napoleon Hill. To some it is part of the *Prosperity Gospel* which is really not a gospel. (Galatians 1:6–9) The *only* Gospel is the D.B.R., death, burial, resurrection, nothing more, and nothing less. (1 Corinthians 15:1–5)

As I see it, this thing they call a paradigm is a biblical principle called the mindset—where your mind is set on something. The question is, what is your mind set on? What is your paradigm? What do you think, speak and act on based on your paradigm?

- PARADIGM (In the Beginning)

The way you think, speak, and do is what determines the life that you live. If you have a positive paradigm, the live you live will be good, but if you have a negative paradigm you will live a life of the walking dead. You will be like the men on death row in the movie *The Green Mile*—dead man walking.

NOTE: Most of the information I am teaching I have gleaned from Bob Proctor and others and then expanded on my own as I prayed and ruminated on the principles. I have added my own insights. I believe the principles on paradigms are biblical as we are called to renew our minds with the Word of God, which in turn will affect the way we think, the way we speak, and the way we live our lives. I am not talking about salvation—how we get saved—but how we live our lives before salvation and after our salvation.

"For by grace you have been saved through faith; and that not of yourselves, it is the gift of God; not as a result of works (or paradigms), so that no one may boast. For we are His workmanship, created

in Christ Jesus for (the purpose) good works, which God prepared beforehand so that we would walk in them."
> ~Ephesians 2:8–10 addition mine

"He saved us, not on the basis of deeds which we have done in righteousness, but according to His mercy, by the washing of regeneration, and renewing by the Holy Spirit."
> ~Titus 3:5

We received nothing by our own goodness, our own works, or good deeds. The same letter written to the church in Galatians that spoke of "another Gospel" (anything that is added to the D.B.R., Death, Burial, Resurrection of Jesus) also speaks of receiving anything apart from faith.

"You foolish Galatians, who has bewitched you, before whose eyes Jesus Christ was publicly portrayed as crucified (on the Cross)? This is the only thing I want to find out from you; did you receive the Spirit by the works of the Law, or by hearing with faith? Are you so foolish? Having begun by the Spirit, are you now being perfected by the flesh? Did you suffer so many things in vain—if indeed it was in vain? So then, does He who provides you with the Spirit and works miracles among you, do it by the works of the Law, or by hearing with faith?
> ~Galatians 3:1–5 addition mine

NOTE: In reference to the principles of paradigms, we are not talking about salvation but working out your own salvation with fear and trembling (Philippians 2:12), renewing your minds with the Word of God, thinking, speaking, and acting based on a shifted paradigm.

I believe that to understand our paradigms, you must understand the makeup of humankind. We are not just a body. We are not just flesh, blood, bones, and visceral organs.

"Now may the God of peace Himself sanctify you entirely; and may

your spirit and soul and body be preserved complete at the coming of our Lord Jesus Christ."

~I Thessalonians 5:23

We are a trifecta of creation which is known as "the crown of creation." We are the highest form of creation there is. We are not on the same level as animals, vegetation, rocks, water. All of those things are part of God's creation, but humans differ in many ways and not just opposable thumbs. We are a human spirit created in the Image of God who has a soul housed in a physical body. We have been given authority and dominion over creation.

Currently, worldwide, there are 7.9+ billion spirits, souls, and bodies—each one with their own specific and, at times, conflicting paradigms.

SPIRIT: pneuma (pnyoo'-mah)=From G4154; a current of air, that is, breath (blast) or a breeze; by analogy or figuratively a spirit, that is, (human) the rational soul, (by implication) vital principle, mental disposition, etc., or (superhuman) an angel, daemon, or (divine) God, Christ's spirit, the Holy spirit: - ghost, life, spirit (-ual, -ually), mind. G4145: pneō (pneh'-o)=A primary word; to breathe hard, that is, breeze: - blow

"The spirit of a person is the lamp of the Lord, Searching all the innermost parts of his being."

~Pro-Verbs 20:27

SOUL: psuchē (psoo-khay')=From G5594; breath, that is, (by implication) spirit, abstractly or concretely (the animal sentient principle only; thus distinguished on the one hand from G4151, which is the rational and immortal soul; and on the other from G2222, which is mere vitality, even of plants. G5594: psuchō (psoo'-kho)=A primary verb; to breathe (voluntarily but gently; thus differing on the one hand from G4154, which denotes properly a forcible respiration; and on the other from the base of G109, which refers properly to an inanimate breeze), that is, (by implication of reduction of temperature by evaporation) to chill (figuratively): - wax cold.

NOTE: The paradigm is connected with the soul, the mind, the volition/free will and our emotions. The negative soul that the carnal, fleshly nature is expressed in, must be shifted.

The word *soul* is used in many positive, cultural ways—*soul* music, *soul* meaning the deep feelings, *soul* food, etc. The soul turns negative when the paradigm (what we feel, what we think, what we say affects how we act) turns negative.

BODY: sōma (so'-mah)=From G4982; the body (as a sound whole), used in a very wide application, literally or figuratively: - bodily, body, slave. G4982: sōzō (sode'-zo)=From a primary word σῶς sōs⁻ (contraction for the obsolete σάος saos, "safe"); to save, that is, deliver or protect (literally or figuratively): - heal, preserve, save (self), do well, be (make) whole.

NOTE: For teaching purposes we can take apart the parts of a human, but in reality, they work synergistically as one unit. Some have described a human being, "We are a spirit who has a soul and who is housed in a body." When our body moves from one place to another the spirit and soul move in concert with our physical being.

- IN THE BEGINNING (Genesis 1:1–31, Genesis 1:26–27, Genesis 2:7, Genesis 2:18–25, Genesis 3:21–3)

This wonderful creation called man and wo-man started in the beginning as part of the creative process.

"In the beginning God created the heavens and the earth."
~Genesis 1:1

CREATED: bârâ› (baw-raw')=A primitive root; (absolutely) to create; (qualified) to cut down (a wood), select, feed (as formative processes): - choose, create (creator), cut down, dispatch, do, make (fat).

NOTE: I believe that God had a thought, an imagination.

He took that thought/imagination and spoke out into the darkness what He was thinking, and the cause and effect was "there was light."

This could be me speculating, but it seem reasonable to me that God has the ultimate paradigm where He thought, He spoke, He acted on His thought, and it was. We were created in the image and likeness of God. We will look closer at the creation of the man and woman (aka Adam and Eve; aka A & E) and see the spirit, soul, and body connection.

NOTE: Take some time and circle all of the words that describe the creative process. Here is my count.

1. God created
2. God said (spoke)
3. God saw
4. God separated
5. God called
6. God made
7. God placed
8. God blessed
9. God gave authority
10. od sanctified
11. God completed
12. God rested

It all started with a desire that became a thought that was spoken and was manifested.

- ENTER MAN AND WO-MAN (Genesis 1:26–27, Genesis 2:7, Genesis 2:18–25)

In the creative process, God had a thought about creating someone in His image and likeness. It appears there was a heavenly board meeting between God and someone else.

"Then God said, let US make man in OUR IMAGE according to (based on) OUR LIKENESS..."
                    ~Genesis 1:26 addition and emphasis mine

IMAGE: tselem (tseh'-lem)=From an unused root meaning to shade; a phantom, that is, (figuratively) illusion, resemblance; hence a representative figure, especially an idol: - image, vain shew.

LIKENESS: demûth (dem-ooth')=From H1819; resemblance; concretely model, shape; adverbially like: - fashion, like (-ness, as), manner, similitude. H1819: dâmâh (daw-maw')=A primitive root; to compare; by implication to resemble, liken, consider: - compare, devise, (be) like (-n), mean, think, use similitudes.

NOTE: The theological speculation that the *us* and the *our* is speaking about God and angelic beings. I don't think so. I think what we are seeing is a reference to the Trinity—God the Father, God the Son (the Word), and God the Holy Spirit. I believe when you look at a human being you are looking the image and likeness of God Himself. Of course, after the fall the perfection was tarnished, thus the need for Jesus on the cross and restoration to factory specifications. I believe also that with the fall—due to high treason and disobedience in the garden—that the paradigm was tarnished.

- INITIAL SPIRIT, SOUL, AND BODY CONNECTION, PARADIGM FOUND (Genesis 2:7)

In Genesis 1:26–27 we see a macro view of the creation of man/wo-man. In Genesis 2:7 we see a micro view—a closer look.

> *"Then the Lord God formed man of dust and the ground and breathed into his nostrils the breath of life and man became a living soul (being)."*
>
> ~Genesis 2:7 addition mine

"We are lumps of clay filled with the glory of God."
~Bruce Coble
Bible Teacher, Pastor, Missionary, my mentor, and my friend

God used the mist rising from the earth that watered the

whole surface of the ground and took dust and made the form of a man (with no life, no animation), including nostrils (nose). God then performed the first know case of C.P.R. (cardiopulmonary resuscitation) and came down low, face to face with the inanimate object and blew His breath into the nostrils of clay. The cause and effect (in my mind) is that the breath (Spirt of God) fill the clay's lungs, and the clay became a living soul. An inanimate object became animated. In my mind I see the body (clay) encounter the Spirit (in man now) and the soul (totality of being including mind, free will, and emotions). I could be wrong but I think I'm right.

NOTE: I believe this is where the first paradigm *on earth as it is in heaven* was created. Man was able to think, speak, and do God thoughts, God words, and God actions. I believe God looked at Adam (remember Eve was not created yet even though the macro view is that God created man—male and female—(Genesis 1:26–27) and said, "He (man) is good." When God looked over all of His creation He said it was *very good.*

"God saw all that He had made, and behold it was VERY GOD..."
~Genesis 1:31 emphasis mine

God had planted a Garden and placed the man (Adam) in the Garden to cultivate and keep His creation. (Genesis 2:15) God then gave freedom in the Garden with one restriction.

"The Lord God commanded the man, saying, from ANY tree of the garden you may eat freely, BUT from the tree of the knowledge of good and evil you shall NOT eat..."
~Genesis 3:16–17 emphasis mine

The cause and effect (consequences) of disobedience (high treason) was death (paradigm lost).

"...for in the day that you eat from it you shall surely die (death)."
~Genesis 3:17 addition mine

NOTE: At this point, the woman (Eve, the mother of all living) has not been created yet.

> *"Then the Lord God said, it is not good for the man to be alone; I will make him a helper suitable for him (apparently animals were not suitable for man)."*
>
>   ~Genesis 2:18–20 addition mine

> *"Out of the ground the Lord God formed every beast of the field and every bird of the sky, and brought them to the man to see what he would call them; and whatever the man called a living creature that was its name. The man gave names to all the cattle, and to the birds of the sky, and to every beast of the field but for Adams there was not found a helper SUITABLE to him."*
>
>   ~Genesis 2:10–20 emphasis mine

NOTE: So much for bestiality (having sex with animals). This would not come until later after the fall and the skewed paradigm (the way a man thinks, speaks and acts). After the fall, when the paradigm was lost, Isaiah 5:20 began.

> *"Woe (judgment is coming) to those who call evil good, and good evil; Who substitute darkness for light and light for darkness; Who substitute bitter for sweet and sweet for bitter!"*
>
>   ~Isaiah 5:20 addition mine

- ENTER THE WOMAN (Genesis 2:21–25)

In these verses we see a lot of firsts take place.
1. The Lord God caused a deep sleep to fall upon the man and he slept (first anesthesiology).
2. Then He gook one of his ribs (first surgery, a ribectomy).
3. The Lord God fashioned into a woman the rib which He had taken from the man (first fashion show).
4. And He brought her to the man (first time the Father walked the bride down the aisle).

5. Then the man said this (woman) is now bone of my bones and flesh of my flesh; she shall be called Woman because she was taken out of man (the first self-written marriage vows).
6. For this reason a man shall leave his father and his mother and be joined to his wife, they shall become one flesh (first pronouncement of marriage and the bride and groom have a honeymoon with sexual relations).
7. The man and his wife (bride) were both naked and were not ashamed (first mention of a bride).

NOTE: At the risk of sounding politically incorrect and insensitive and not being woke, "in the beginning" marriage and sexual relations was between a man and a woman and not between beast (animals), little children, between a man and man or woman and woman. This would come later after the fall in the garden, and the man and woman's paradigm was perverted. The relationship was between Adam and Eve and not Adam and Steve.

> "This book of the law shall not depart from your mouth, but you shall meditate on it day and night, so that you may be careful to do according to all that is written in it; for then you will make your way prosperous and then you will have (good) success."
>
> ~Joshua 1:8 addition mine

CHAPTER TEN

PARADIGM LOST
THE GARDEN TEMPTATION, THE FALL, ORIGINAL SIN, PARADIGM LOST

The paradigm originally in the image of God was about to be shifted (from good to bad) and would need to be shifted back into the original state (from bad to good). The male and female, man and woman, Adam and Eve had the Word of God, they had authority, and they had a free will. They were about to be tempted, and what they choose would change the course of history.

> *"Now the serpent was more crafty than any beast of the field which the Lord God had made. And he said to the woman, indeed has God said, you shall not eat from any tree of the garden?"*
>
> ~Genesis 3:1

NOTE: The serpent crept into the Garden, because he was a creep. Both the man and the woman were given authority and dominion over every animal including the creepers—those who moved. (Genesis 1:26–27, 30)

NOTE: Temptation is not designed to pull you into evil sin, but it is designed to pull you away from who you really are and your destiny. He did it to Adam and Eve, he did it to people in the Old Testament, he did it to Jesus in the wilderness, and he does it to you and me.

What was the first question from the serpent (the creep) to the woman? (Genesis 3:1)

What answer did the woman give to the serpent (the creep)? (Genesis 3:2–3)

NOTE: At this point the creep is putting doubt in the woman's paradigm. "Indeed, has God said…" (Genesis 3:1) Today, in the 21st century, the creep is still using the same techniques with us, putting doubt into our paradigm/mind. He is saying things like, "Indeed has God said it is His will for you to be healed?" "Indeed has God said that He wishes you to prosper and be in health even as your soul prospers?" "Indeed has God said that He wants to give you an abundant life?" Once the doubt is planted in the mind, then you begin to think, speak, and act based on what the creep has lied about.

Notice that even though the woman was created after the man and the original orders given to the man, were known by the woman. Apparently, Adam passed the command on down to Eve.

What did the serpent, the creep say about God's command? (Genesis 3:4)

NOTE: Not only did the serpent place doubt in the woman's mind about what God said, he then put doubt in the mind about God being truthful about that death thing.

What reason did the serpent give the woman about why God told them about the things God said? (Genesis 3:5)

NOTE: The seeds for sin were planted. The seeds for a negative paradigm were planted.

What three things did the woman see? (Genesis 3:6) I believe that these three things correlate with all that is in the world today. (1 John 1:16)

What are the three things that correlate with the three things in the garden that the woman saw? (Genesis 3:6, 1 John 1:16)

What did the woman do when she took from the tree's fruit and ate? (Genesis 3:6)

NOTE: The woman gets blamed for all of the world's problems because of her disobedience to the Word of God. I find it interesting that the man was standing right next to the woman as she gave fruit also to her husband WITH her, and he ate. (Genesis 3:6) Later on we see that the responsibility for what happened in the garden was on the shoulders of the man—who had authority to tell the creep to get out, as did the woman.

"Therefore, as sin came into the world through one man (Adam), and death as the result of sin (disobedience), so death (separation of fellowship with God and physical death) spread to all men, [no one being able to stop it or to escape its power] because all men sinned."
~Romans 5:12 AMP with emphasis and additions mine
Ruminator Style

NOTE: I believe that it at this moment not only was death introduced to the world, but that was the moment that the paradigm shifted from the original paradigm to paradigm lost.

- ## THE CAUSE AND EFFECT OF DISOBEDIENCE/ HIGH TREASON

What was open for both Adam and Eve? (Genesis 3:7)

What did they both know? (Genesis 3:7)

NOTE: Their thinking was changed. There was a change in their paradigm, the thought which affected their actions. There speech was changed also as they began to speak blame and shame.

What action did they take? (Genesis 3:7)

NOTE: This is the beginning of the cover-up. With their new way of thinking, they realized that they needed to cover up. They took the leaves that God had created and tried to hide the cause and effect of their original sin.

What did A & E hear? (Genesis 3:8)

What time of day did they hear God walking? (Genesis 3:8)

From what did they hid themselves from? (Genesis 3:8)

PRESENCE OF THE LORD: pânîym (paw-neem') =the face (as the part that turns); against, anger, X as (long as), at, + battle, + because (of), + beseech, countenance, edge, + employ, endure, + enquire, face, favour, fear of, for, forefront (-part), form (-er time, -ward), from, front, heaviness, X him (-self), + honorable, + impudent, + in presence, prospect, was purposed, by reason, of, + regard, right forth, + serve, X showbread, sight, state, straight, X street, X thee, X

them (-selves), through (+ -out), till, time (-s) past, (un-) to (-ward),
+ upon, upside (+ down), with (-in, + stand), X ye, X you.

NOTE: Sin elicits the same response of hiding from the presence
of the Lord, like Jonah.

> *"But Jonah got up to flee to Tarshish from the presence of the
> LORD. So he went down to Joppa, found a ship that was going to
> Tarshish, paid the fare, and boarded it to go with them to Tarshish
> away from the presence of the LORD."*
>
> ~Jonah 1:3

What did God do? (Genesis 3:9)
What was Adam's response to the calling of God? (Genesis 3:10)
What was God's question? (Genesis 3:11)
NOTE: Adam's response was from his new paradigm. This is the
beginning of the *blame game*.
When Adam began the blame game, he went for the twofer.
1. The woman
2. that You (God) gave me.
When the tables turned to Eve, she joined in to the blame game
as she pulled a *Flip Wilson*—the comedian famous for saying, *the
devil made me do it*. She admitted that she had been deceived, "…
the serpent deceived me and I ate."
It was at this point that God turned to the serpent and began the
pronouncement of the curse.

• THE CURSE (Genesis 3:14–19)

The Serpent/D-Evil (Genesis 3:14–15)
a. Cursed more than all cattle and more than every best of the
field. This was because of what the d-evil had done (tempted A & E)
b The serpent would go on his belly (it seems that the serpent
had legs that he crept in with) all the days of your life.
c. Enmity would be put between the serpent's seed and the woman's seed.

d. He (Jesus) shall bruise you (the serpent/d-evil) on the head and you (the d-evil) shall bruise Him (Jesus) on the heel.

NOTE: This is a Messianic prophesy speaking of Jesus on the cross with the d-evil's head being bruised (authority over death and the d-evil) and the d-evil bruising the heel (the death of Jesus). Jesus dealt with the curse on the tree/cross to restore blessing and I think the lost paradigm. (Genesis 3:10–14, 1 Corinthians 15:1–5)

The Woman (Genesis 3:16)
  a. I will greatly multiply your pain in childbirth.
  b. In pain you shall bring forth children.
  c. Your desire shall be for your husband in spite of the pain in childbirth.

The Man (Genesis 3:17–19)
  a. Cursed is the ground
  b. In toil you shall eat of it all the days of your life.
  c. Both thorns and thistles shall grow for you.
  d. You shall eat of the plant of field.
  d. By the sweat of your face/brow you shall eat bread.
  e. You will return to the ground (dust) because from it you were taken (clay)
  f. For you are dust and to dust you shall return (death)
  g. You will be driven out of the Garden and prevented from returning back to the garden in case he returns to eat from the tree of life and live forever in the sin state.
  h. The man was sent from the garden and cultivate the (cursed) ground from which he was taken.

NOTE: The man and the woman now were thinking from a different paradigm. They were thinking from a blessed paradigm to a cursed paradigm, and that paradigm would be passed on down through the centuries. Romans 5:12 speaks of this paradigm shift that was passed on to the billions of people who would be born with the sin DNA defect in their lives.

"Therefore, just as through one man (Adam and Eve) sin (paradigm

shift) entered into the world and death through sin, and so death spread to all men (mankind) because all sinned."
~Romans 5:12 with emphasis and additions mine,
Ruminator Style

NOTE: The original command to Adam (later passed on to Eve) was that:

"for in THE DAY that you eat from it you SHALL SURELY DIE."
~Genesis 2:17 emphasis mine

We see that they did not drop over dead immediately. They ate, the curse was pronounced, and the beginning of death was set into motion by their disobedience/high treason. From then until now the effects of the curse are manifested. There needed to be something that would *reverse the curse,* and that something was Jesus. I believe that act of disobedience affects all mankind with the curse, the physical, spiritual, mental, and emotional nature of mankind. The paradigm of fear, doubt, unbelief, was set into motion. Mankind needed not only a Savior for their sin nature, but we also needed a paradigm shift in the way that we think, speak, and act. Over and over we see the fallen paradigm imagination thought about, spoken about, and acted upon.

"And Jehovah saw that the wickedness of man was great in the earth, and that every imagination of the thoughts of his heart was only evil continually."
~Genesis 6:5

"Woe to those who call evil good, and good evil; Who substitute darkness for light and light for darkness; Who substitute bitter for sweet and sweet for bitter!"
~Isaiah 5:20

We see how the high treason of disobedience affected the world. In Genesis 11:1–9 we see the connection between what is thought (imagined), what is spoken (language) and what is done (acted upon).

What was the whole earth using? (Genesis 11:1)

When the people settled in the land of Shinar what did they say to one another? (Genesis 11:1)

3. What did they use for stone and mortar? (Genesis 11:3)

NOTE: Bricks and tar were substitutes for stones and mud. One is manmade the other is God-made.

What did they say was the reason for the substituted materials? (Genesis 11:4)

What was the purpose of the manmade tower? (Genesis 11:4)

What did they want to make for themselves? (Genesis 11:4)

What was their concern if they did not make a name for themselves? (Genesis 11:4)

What did the Lord come down for? (Genesis 11:5)

What did the Lord see that the people had? (Genesis 11:6)

What would the cause and effect be as the one people had the same language? (Genesis 11:6)

NOTE: They has one language/word, one intent/purpose. I believe that they had one paradigm.

What did they (Us) go down and do? (Genesis 11: 7)

What was the purpose of confusing the language? (Genesis 11: 7)

What was the cause and effect of the scattering? (Genesis 11:8)

What was the name given the land of Shinar? (Genesis 11:8)

Why was it called Babel (bay bull) (Genesis 11:9)

How did the Lord do? (Genesis 11:9)

NOTE: I believe what happened to the people of Babel is what happened to Job.

"For the thing which I greatly feared is come upon me, and that which I was afraid of is come unto me."

~Job 3:25

"...let us make a name for ourselves a name, otherwise we will be scattered abroad over the face of the earth."

~Genesis 11:4, 9

NOTE: What they thought, what they spoke, and how they acted resulted in exactly what their paradigm manifested in their lives. The same thing happens to us in our fallen paradigm conditions. We must have a paradigm shift.

In our next chapter we will see the only way to have a paradigm shift which will affect the way we make our way prosperous and how we will have good (not bad) success.

> *"This book of the law shall not depart from your mouth, but you shall meditate on it day and night so that you may be careful to do according to all that is written in it; for then you will make your way prosperous and then you will have (good) success."*
>
> ~Joshua 1:8 addition mine

CHAPTER ELEVEN

PARADIGM FOUND (SHIFTED)

We have seen the Paradigm in its original condition, and then we saw the Paradigm Lost, and now we look at the Paradigm Found. The original paradigm was connected with the Creator of the Universe. I believe that in its original state, the paradigm was one of intimacy with God, true fellowship (connection with God), and the roots of true prosperity and success. When Adam and Eve committed high treason by disobedience, mankind entered into a state of poverty and failure.

To have a true Paradigm Shift back to the original state to the point of blessing and not a curse, there needs to be a propitiation (satisfactory substitute) for God. That shift will be with the restoration and redemption of mankind. That sacrifice will be a bloody Jesus on the cross who would die, who would be buried, and on the 3rd day be raised from the dead. (1 Corinthians 15:1–5, Galatians 2:20, Hebrews 9:22)

Even after the reset to the original state, we will still need to have daily renewing of the mind, daily paradigm shifting so we can think faith, speak faith, and act upon faith so that we can have prosperity and (good) success.

"As a man thinketh in his heart so he is."

~Pro-Verbs 23:7

"…out of the abundance of the heart the mouth speaks."
~Luke 6:45
"For there is no good tree which produces bad fruit nor, on the other hand, a bad tree which produces good fruit. For each tree is

*known by its own fruit. For men do not gather figs from thorns,
nor do they pick grapes from a briar bush. The good man out of the
good treasure of his heart brings forth what is good; and the evil
man out of the evil treasure (of his heart) brings forth what is evil;
for his mouth speaks from that which fills his heart."*

~Luke 6:43–45 addition mine

NOTE: Notice the connection between the mind, the heart, and
the mouth. This is the paradigm where we think, we speak, and we act.

NOTE: Take note that in the original state the paradigm was in
a garden filled with trees and fruit (Genesis 2:15–16), the fall in the
garden took place with trees and fruit that was eaten in the garden
(Genesis 3: 1–19),the restoration is found also with a tree.

- Who is under a curse? (Galatians 3:10, Deuteronomy 27:26)
- Who is justified by the Law before God? (Galatians 3:11, Habakkuk 2:4, Galatians 2:16, Romans 1:17, Hebrews 10:38)
- Is the law of faith? (Galatians 3:12)
- What shall the one who practices the Law do? (Galatians 3:12, Leviticus 18:5)
- Who redeemed us from the curse of the law? (Galatians 3:13)
- How did Christ redeem us (pay the price) from the curse of the Law? (Galatians 3:13, Deuteronomy 21:23, Galatians 4:5)
- What did Christ become for us? (Galatians 3:13)
- Who is cursed? (Galatians 3:13, Deuteronomy 21:23, Acts 5:30)
- What was the cause and effect of Christ becoming a curse on the tree/cross? (Galatians 3:14)
- What comes on the Gentiles? (Galatians 3:14)
- What would the Gentiles receive when the blessings of Abraham comes on them? (Galatians 3:14)

NOTE: Check out the Blessings found in Deuteronomy 28 and
Deuteronomy 29 for a listing of the Curses and Blessings.

NOTE: The soul is made up of the mind (what we think), the will
(our free choices), and our emotions (the indicator of our feelings).
The free will that God gave Adam and Eve in the Garden is the
same free will that we had before we accepted the Lord, and the

same free will that we daily choose as we live out our lives. I believe that our free will is pivotal in our choice to follow God, to walk in blessings, and how we shift our paradigms.

"I call heaven and earth to witness against you today, that I have set before you, life and death, the blessing and the curse. So choose life in order that you may live, you and your descendants."

~Deuteronomy 30:19

NOTE: The choice you make (choose wisely my friends) will not only affect you but your descendants. Our paradigms will be passed down to our children. There must be a paradigm shift, if not for our sake, for the sake of our children. The paradigm is formed pre-birth with sin, familial D.N.A., and post-birth by our family and their traditions, school systems, peers, the media, which shapes and molds the way that we think, speak, and act. Not all of the original paradigm is bad, but if not shifted (renewed) it will shape and create our future and will be passed down to our children and children's children (our grandchildren).

NOTE: Instead of a Curse Paradigm we have the authority and ability to shift into a Blessing Paradigm where we think, speak, and act blessed instead of being cursed which in turn will be prosperous and successful.

The paradigm lost is under the control of sin (Romans 3:10, Romans 3:23) however the hope is that there is a righteousness by faith. (Romans 1:17) Between Romans 3:10 and Romans 1:17 something happens that shifts the paradigm and our lives. That is 2 Corinthians 5:21.

"He (God the Father) made Him (Jesus) who knew no sin to be sin on our behalf so that we might become the righteousness of God in Him."

~2 Corinthians 5:21 addition mine

"Therefore IF any person is [engrafted] in Christ (the Anointed One anointed with yoke breaking, burden lifting, oppression

removing healing power of the Holy Ghost) he is a new creation
(with a new paradigm) (a new creature altogether); the old (man,
paradigm) [previous moral and spiritual condition] has passed
away. Behold, the fresh and new (man, paradigm) has come (and
is constantly coming)."

~2 Corinthians 5:17 AMP, emphasis and additions mine

Ruminator Style

Once we are born again, anew, afresh, from above (John 3:3–6)
we are a new creation, (2 Corinthians 5:17) however, we are a work
in progress. The good work is started in us that God will continue
in us until Jesus returns. (Philippians 1:6). Until Jesus returns we are
to work out our own salvation with fear and trembling. (Philippians
2:12) We can be free, but in our freedom we can be bound again if
we don't keep standing firm and don't be subject again to a yoke of
slavery. (Galatians 5:1, 13, 16)

NOTE: For us to stay free, we must take control over what we
think, what we speak, and what we do. There is a principle of the
Kingdom called sowing and reaping which goes hand in hand with
a the natural laws called cause and effect.

"Do not be deceived, God is not mocked, for whatever (no limits)
a man sows, this he will also reap. For the one who sows to his own
flesh will from the flesh reap corruption, but the one who sows to
the Spirit reap eternal life."

~Galatians 6:7–8 addition mine

• THE RENEWED PARADIGM

A paradigm is merely a mindset that will change the trajectory of
your life. A renewed paradigm will be the difference between death
and life and peace. The only way to reset your paradigm is by your
free will to renew your mind with the Word of God. Hand in hand
with that renewed mind is thinking positive things, speaking positive
things, and acting based on what you think and speak. What you
put out in the world with your words and actions is what will come

back to you. It is the sowing and reaping principle where you can sow poison ivy or corn. Both will reproduce and give a harvest. The seed that you sow will be with your mouth.

"Now the mind set (an action, verb) resulting in a mindset (a paradigm) on the flesh (the carnal nature) is death (separation from God), BUT (in contrast) the mind set (an action, verb) resulting in a mindset (a paradigm) on the Spirit (Holy) is life (and that more abundantly, aka Abundant Life) and peace (rest and wholeness)."
~Romans 8:6 emphasis and additions mine
Ruminator Style

NOTE: These last three chapters have been a thumbnail sketch of Paradigms. I have spent a lot of time on Paradigms because I believe it is critical to Biblical Prosperity and Success, having enough to meet your needs and an overflow to meet the needs of others and to accomplish the purposes of God in your life.

"This book of the Law (the Word of God, His thoughts, His wishes and desires for you) shall not depart from your mouth (as you mutter under your breath what His word says) but you shall meditate (ruminate, think about, mull over in your mind as you speak His Word out loud) on it (the Law, the Word) day and night (7/24/365, all the time with every circumstance in your life) SO (the reason for meditation/rumination) that you (insert your name) may be careful to do (action on your part based on what you think and say) according to (based on) all that is written in it (the Law, the Word); for then (cause and effect) you (not God or not anyone else) will make (produce) your way (the way that you walk and live out your life) prosperous (enough to meet your needs and overflow to help others) and then (cause and effect of being prosperous) you (fill in your name) will have (cause and effect) have (good) success (accomplishing the purposes of God in your life).
~Joshua 1:8 emphasis and additions mine
Ruminator Style

CHAPTER TWELVE

COMMUNICATING WITH PEOPLE

Communication is one of the main keys to prosperity and success. Communication is connecting with someone, whether it be in the business world or with interpersonal connections. Without good communication we will never have prosperity or success. Oh, you may build a *building,* but if it is built on shifting sands, your prosperity and success will fall—and fall hard. At the risk of sounding redundant, I will be covering some of the same information again because I believe repetition is the key to learning. The apostle Paul believed the same thing.

> *"Finally, my brothers and sisters, rejoice in the Lord. To write the same things again is no trouble for me, and it is a safeguard for you"*
> ~Philippians 3:1

In the following chapters, we will talk about Communicating with God to have Biblical Prosperity and Success.

COMMUNICATION: (1) the act or process of communicating; fact of being communicated. (2) the imparting or interchange of thoughts, opinions, or information by speech, writing, or signs. (3) something imparted, interchanged, or transmitted. (4) a document or message imparting news, views, information, etc. (5) passage, or an opportunity or means of passage, between places.

COMMUNICATIONS: (1) means of sending messages, orders, etc., including telephone, telegraph, radio, and television. (2) routes and transportation for moving troops and supplies from a base to an area of operations.

Currently the census of the world is 7.9+ billion people, give or take a few due to new births and deaths. There are 6,500 languages and dialects spoken in the world today.

Each language represent a human being who communicates with other human beings in some from or fashion. Communication is the ability to interact with other people on some level. The bottom line for communication are words expressed verbally, written, gestures, body posture, and countenance (expressions on the face).

In the Bible the word for communication is koinonia (koy-nohn-ee'-ah) which has multiple meanings including fellowship, social intercourse, sharing something in common, communication, communion.

COMMUNICATION: koinōnia (koy-nohn-ee'-ah)=From G2844; partnership, that is, (literally) participation, or (social) intercourse, or (pecuniary) benefaction: - (to) communicate (-ation), communion, (contri-), distribution, fellowship. G2844: koinōnos (koy-no-nos')=- From G2839; a sharer, that is, associate: - companion, X fellowship, partaker, partner. G839: koinos (koy-nos')= common, that is, (literally) shared by all or several, or (ceremonially) profane: - common, defiled, unclean, unholy.

Communication can be negative or positive. It can be constructive or destructive. Communication can be one-way or two-way. Communication can tear down fences and walls or build fences and walls, depending on your PARADIGM—the way you think, speak, and act towards one another.

NOTE: In the next chapter we will see that communication with God is not a monologue—you talking and asking but never hearing from God—but it is a dialogue, where God talks, and you listen, and then you talk, and God listens. The Word of God—also known as *The Manufacturer's Handbook*, a term coined by scientist and author Harold Hill—is also the *Codebook of Communication*, a term coined by me.

• WHAT IS A PARADIGM?

A paradigm is merely the way that you think, which affects the way you communicate, resulting in the way you act. You will either react negatively or respond positively. There are 7.9 +billion paradigms in the world.

A paradigm starts way before you were ever born—and in fact way before your parents were born. Your paradigm was started before you were a glimmer in your parent's eyes, before they fell in love, got married, had sexual intercourse (of course in these days the order may not be in that manner), and then nine months—approximately 280 days—later after the coming together of the sperm and the egg, you made your appearance on planet earth communicate loudly with your new world. Everything that your parents did physically—drink, smoke, eat right, do drugs, exercise, etc.—and the life various choices they made was passed down to you genetically Your paradigm was kick started. And that includes all your genetic ancestors, all the way back into The Garden of Eden where Adam and Eve choose to commit high treason by disobedience—all of that was passed down to all man and woman-kind.

> *"Therefore, just as through one man (Adam/Eve) sin entered into the world, and death through sin, and so death spread/passed to ALL men, because all sinned."*
> ~Romans 5:12 additions and emphasis mine,
> Ruminator Style

This is why the Bible tells us,

> *"…there is none righteous (meeting the standard of God) no not one."*
> ~Roman 3:10 addition mine

> *"…for all have sinned and fall short of the glory (light/presence) of God."*
> ~Romans 3:23 addition mine

There is a solution which will restore us to our ORIGINAL PAR-ADIGM state from before the fall. This is why we see that between the point of all sinning (Romans 3:10, Romans 3:23), and "the righteous walk by faith," 2 Corinthians 5:17 took place.

> *"Therefore IF any person (or Paradigm) is IN CHRIST (the Anointed One/Messiah and His anointing that breaks the yoke (Isaiah 26:10, Isaiah 58:6, Acts 10:38) he is a NEW CREATION (a new creature altogether); the OLD [previous, moral and spiritual condition] has passed away. Behold, the FRESH and NEW has come!"*
> ~2 Corinthians 5:17 AMP with emphasis and addition mine
> Ruminator Style

This initial paradigm is called NATURE. Then NURTURE kicks in as your family traditions and habits are poured into you (aka familial), influences from your school (what they teach you, good, bad, or ugly), your friends (who have their own paradigms in play), social media (filled with multiple opinions and influences) affect you with a combination of negative/positive influences. Nurture is also called environmental influences.

NOTE: Jesus came and restore the original paradigm by dealing with A & E missing the mark. However, while there is restoration to original intent, we still must deal with our souls, the way we think, choices we make and the way we act emotionally.

• WHO YOU ARE AS A HUMAN BEING

There are 7.9+ billion people living on Planet Earth with 7.9+ billion paradigms and modes of communication. Not all of those people have encountered a life-changing experience with Jesus. We are called to present them with the opportunity to choose life. How we communicate with them could make the difference between them accepting Jesus or rejecting Jesus. Sometimes, I think they don't reject Jesus, but they reject Christians with a negative paradigm. To communicate effectively, I believe that we as Christians need to have a PARADIGM SHIFT in the way we think, the way we speak, the way we act, and yes, the way we communicate.

- THE MAKE UP OF 7.9+ BILLION PEOPLE ON PLANET EARTH

"And may the God of peace Himself sanctify you through and through [separate you from profane things, make you pure and wholly consecrated to God]; and may your spirit and soul and body be preserved sound and compete [and found] blameless at the coming of our Lord Jesus Christ (the Messiah)."
~I Thessalonians 5:23 AMP

"In the beginning…"
~Genesis 1:1

The God of the created universe, created the world and all that is in it.

"…and it was GOOD."
~Genesis 1:10, 12, 18, 21, 25 emphasis mine

"And God saw all that He had made, and behold, it was VERY GOOD…"
~Genesis 1:31 emphasis mine

NOTE: Too many people worship the universe and not the Creator of the universe, which eventually ends up in the worship of themselves in the Church of It's All About Me Baby, aka humanism.

NOTE: When I think about my roots, I have to say in my best T.L. Osborne (Pentecostal preacher and author of the classic book *Healing the Sick*) voice or in my best Pentecostal preacher voice, or in my best blues singer voice, "Goood Gawd, yawl!"

The blueprint for human beings started with two proto-types, a male and a female, man and wo-man, Adam and Eve. Once again, they were "very good."

"Then God said, Let US make man in OUR IMAGE and in OUR LIKENESS..."

~Genesis 1:26 emphasis mine

"God created man in HIS OWN IMAGE, in the IMAGE OF GOD He created him; male and female, He created them."

~Genesis 1:27 emphasis mine

NOTE: I believe that the "Us" and "Our" was not angels but Jesus,

"In the beginning was the Word and the Word was with God and the Word WAS GOD...and the Word became FLESH and dwelt among us and we beheld His glory as that of the only begotten from the Father, full of grace and truth."

~John 1:1, 14 emphasis mine

Jesus was THE WORD in the beginning. The third person who was involved in the creation was the Spirit of God, the Holy Spirit, the Holy Ghost (Genesis 1:2)

NOTE: I believe that the initial creation of the male and female became the blueprint for you and me. At this point the paradigm was good, it was in the image and likeness of God, it was blessed, it had directives to be fruitful and multiply, fill the earth and subdue (have dominion/authority over the earth) it. This initial paradigm was filled with God-thoughts, God-words and God-actions. With the fall of disobedience and high treason (due to man's volition and free will) the paradigm was skewed and needed to have a PARDAIGM SHIFT which came with the D.B.R., death, burial, and resurrection of Jesus. After the restoration, the paradigm had to be constantly recalibrated, shifted, and changed in correlation with the renewing of the mind by the Word of God.

NOTE: Many people try to shift and change their paradigm by their own goodness, positive thoughts, doing good things which is really fine, however it will never meet the full potential that we are designed for, and there will always be a constant conflict of communication with the world.

• CREATION OF THE SPIRIT, SOUL, AND BODY

SPIRIT (pneuma, little s, human spirit)

SOUL (psyche, psyche, the totality of man, the mind, the free will/choice and the emotions)

BODY (soma, clay vessel, flesh, blood and bones, the housing/temple of the Holy Ghost, the carrier of the spirit and soul)

"Then the Lord God FORMED man of dust from the ground/clay and BREATHE into his nostrils the BREATH OF LIFE and man BECAME a LIVING SOUL."
~Genesis 2:7 emphasis mine

"We are just lumps of clay filled with the glory of God."
~Bruce Coble

SPIRIT: pneuma (pnyoo'-mah)=From G4154; a current of air, that is, breath (blast) or a breeze; by analogy or figuratively a spirit, that is, (human) the rational soul, (by implication) vital principle, mental disposition, etc., or (superhuman) an angel, daemon, or (divine) God, Christ's spirit, the Holy spirit: - ghost, life, spirit (-ual, -ually), mind. G4154: pneō (pneh'-o)=A primary word; to breathe hard, that is, breeze: - blow.

"The spirit of a person is the lamp of the LORD, Searching all the innermost parts of his being."
~Pro–Verbs 20:27

NOTE: A clay lamp is filled with oil, and when the wick is lit there is illumination. I believe within the human spirit is where the Holy Spirit dwells and is the communication center with the Creator of the universe where we serve the Lord first before we ever serve Him outwardly (Roman 1:9).

I believe this is where The Holy Spirit returns after being in the presence of the Lord and knows how to pray through us according to the will of God (Romans 8:26–28). I believe this is where the fruit (of the Spirit) grows (Galatians 5:22–23) and the gifts (of the Spirit) flow (1 Corinthians 12:1–11). I believe the lamp of the Lord is where we declare that Jesus is Lord first and then with the body/mouth (1 Corinthians 12:3, Romans 10:6–10). I believe this is where we believe in our hearts that Jesus is Lord (Romans 10:9). When you live in a dark world, you become the light of the world as Jesus the Light of the world shines within you, your lamp, your little s, your human spirit (Matthew 5:14–16).

SOUL: psuchē (psoo-khay')=From G5594; breath, that is, (by implication) spirit, abstractly or concretely (the animal sentient principle only; thus distinguished on the one hand from G4151, which is the rational and immortal soul; and on the other from G2222, which is mere vitality, even of plants: these terms thus exactly correspond respectively to the Hebrew G5594: psuchō (psoo'-kho)=A primary verb; to breathe (voluntarily but gently; thus differing on the one hand from G4154, which denotes properly a forcible respiration; and on the other from the base of G109, which refers properly to an inanimate breeze), that is, (by implication of reduction of temperature by evaporation) to chill (figuratively): - wax cold.

NOTE: The soul is considered to be our (a) mind (b) will (c) emotions. In the Hebrew language the soul is the totality of who we are, but in the Greek it is broken down. Our minds are what we think, our will is our volition or free will to choose based on what we think, and our emotions are the gauge for how we feel (joy/depression/anger etc. I believe that our PARADIGMS are formed here. Remember that our BRAINS are not our minds, but merely the switching station that tells thoughts, nerves, and actions what to do and how to react in the flesh or respond in the Spirit. It is the soul, the mind, the paradigm that must be renewed by the Word of God.

> "Unrestrained thoughts (what we think) produces unrestrained words (what we say/communicate) resulting in unrestrained actions (what we do)."
>
> How to Discipline the Flesh by Kenneth Copeland
> with emphasis and additions mine, Ruminator Style

"Without restrained thoughts, words, and actions, you have chaos."
~Rodfucious

NOTE: We always hear that the Lord saves our souls, however I believe that it is more likely that our spirits are saved, our souls are renewed, and our bodies decay. Eventually, all three will be collected for heaven.

NOTE: The soul is under our control. We can tell our souls what to think, how to act, and what to feel. If you remember, when you accepted Jesus and He saved you, you still could choose to walk in the flesh (carnal nature) and be bound again by sin. Depending on our paradigm we can bless the Lord, grumble and complain, praise and be raised, complain and remain, etc.

NOTE: I believe that you can tell if someone has a negative paradigm by the words they speak, by their actions toward other human beings, and by what and who is attracted to their lives. Have you ever known anyone who lives in constant drama, is constantly emotionally unstable, is constantly walking around like Eeyore with a cloud over their heads, and then they blame everybody and every-thing bad on luck or karma or other people? Some people justify their sins due to the d-evil, their lot in life, etc. Brenda and I some-times will hear people talking negatively, or we see their lives fall apart, and we look at each other and say at the same time, "Negative paradigm." We look at the news and see the world falling apart in these DARK DAZES in this PANDEMIC OF FEAR fueled by SYSTEMIC SIN (not just racism) manifested by SYSTEMIC HATE (lack of communication) with the SYSTEMIC ROOTS OF BITTERNESS wrapping around the hearts and minds of the world, and think, NEGATIVE PARADIGM.

BODY: sōma (so'-mah)=From G4982; the body (as a sound whole), used in a very wide application, literally or figuratively: - bodily, body, slave. G4982: sōzō (sode'-zo)=From a primary word σῶς sōs (con-traction for the obsolete σάος saos, "safe"); to save, that is, deliver or protect (literally or figuratively): - heal, preserve, save (self), do well, be (make) whole.

NOTE: The body is the housing unit that hold the spirit and the soul. The human body carries out the will of the Father on earth as it is in heaven. The human body is what communicates with other human bodies. When you combine the words psuche/psyche (soul) with the soma (the body) you get the words psychosomatic which means that the soul/paradigm affects the physicality of the body. Many are sick because their paradigm is sick, which in turns affect the spirit and your relationship with God.

> *"Do you not know that you are a temple of God and that the Spirit of God dwells in you? If any man destroys the temple of God, God will destroy him for the temple of God is holy, and that is what you are?"*
>
> ~1 Corinthians 3:16, 17

> *"Flee immorality, every other sin that man commits is outside the body, but the immoral man sins against his own body. Or do you not know that your body is a temple of the Holy Spirit who is IN YOU whom you have from God, and that you are not your own? For you have been bought with a price; therefore glorify God in your body."*
>
> ~1 Corinthians 6:18–20 emphasis mine

There you have it—you are a triune being who, when connected with God synergistically, functions with a purpose to glorify God, the reason that we were created.

> *"Thou art worthy, O Lord, to receive glory and honor and power: for thou hast created all things, and for thy pleasure they are and were created.*
>
> ~Revelation 4:11

- COMMUNICATION OF A SPIRIT, SOUL, AND BODY TO ANOTHER SPIRIT, AND SOUL, AND BODY

Wow, that was a lot of groundwork covered to talk about how to communicate with people. I teach others in my profession and also nurses, doctors, etc. that we got into business to treat and serve people. The problem is that we become motivated and driven by money and profit. I know when I first started as a Speech-Language Pathologist, I worked at a Rehabilitation Hospital where we saw the sickest of sick patients. We were able to treat the patient until the patient was healed totally or they truly reached their maximum potential. We were able to see the patient, with all disciplines involved, for a year or more. In this day and age, you may be allowed to see the patient for seven weeks, one discipline from calendar episode, and then you must get out. This is true for hospitals, home health, and rehab centers.

I remember when an early mentor of mine told me, when I was not going to pick up a young lady for treatment, who had a traumatic brain injury, "Rodney, NEVER put anyone on the back burner."

That stuck with me for 31 years. I have treated patients who have had rehab before, and everyone from doctors to therapists have given up on the patient—but they made significant improvement when I saw them for treatment again.

The biggest lesson I have been taught by the Lord and which I have taught students, caregivers, doctors, nurses, etc. is TREAT THE WHOLE MAN/WOMAN. Don't just go in and do the physical things, but touch people in their spirit, in their soul and then in their body. The first two will have an effect on the body.

I believe this same principle applies with communication (whether just relating to a human or witnessing to a non-Christian), COM-MUNICATE WITH THE WHOLE MAN/WOMAN.

We are connecting, communicating with a person and not just a non-descript individual.

If you have a mindset that the person is a dirty, rotten, hell-bound sinner and you hate that person (that is the ultimate bad paradigm) then you can NEVER connect with them.

NOTE: At this time many are saying to themselves out loud, "Rodney, I don't hate anyone one! I hate the sin and not the sinner!" I know that sounds good and justifies your hate, but it breaks the communication connection with them. Remember that word, *koinonia*? It has many meanings, but for believers it is fellowship between other believers that we can NEVER have with non-Christians, but we can connect with communication.

FINAL THOUGHTS…FINALLY

Love is the motivator for communication with others, especially with the non-Christian. Minister in love to the whole person. You can have faith but if you don't have love you have nothing.

"And though I have the gift of prophecy, and understand all mysteries and all knowledge, and though I have all faith, so that I could remove mountains, but have not love, I am nothing."

~1 Corinthians 13:1

"For in Christ Jesus neither circumcision nor uncircumcision means anything, but faith working through love. For God did not send the Son into the world to judge/condemn the world, but that the world might be save through Him."

~John 3:17

"Or do you think highly of the riches of His kindness and tolerance and patience, you knowing that the kindness of God leads to repentance."

~Romans 2:4

"But God demonstrates (shows us how to do it) His own love towards us in that while we were YET sinners, Christ died for us."
~Romans 5:8 emphasis and addition mine

- FINAL THOUGHTS…FINALLY…YES FOR REAL THIS TIME

I believe that the God who so love the world (not just Christians) has the ultimate word on motivation for us to treat and communicate with people. That word is LOVE.

"For God (the Creator) so loved (was motivated) the world (all of the 7.9+ Billion current people and all who have died) that He

gave (action) His only begotten Son (Jesus, the most precious thing He had) that WHOSOEVER (no limit to who can benefit from His love) BELIEVES (trusts in, clings to, relies on, adheres to, and clings to) in His (the Father's) only begotten (unique) Son will NOT perish but have everlasting/eternal life."

~John 3:16 emphasis and addition min

Jesus, the one who came to fulfill the Law (principles) of God and not destroy the Law, was asked by a religious person (who had a religious paradigm) what was the "foremost of all." Here is the extrapolation of Jesus' answer (to which the religious was in agreement with Jesus on His answer). Jesus says in Mark 12:29–31:

1. The Lord is ONE God (not multiple gods)
2. Love the Lord your God with all your (1) heart (2) soul (3) mind (4) strength
3. Love your neighbor
4. Love your neighbor as you love yourself.

NOTE: I believe that we cannot connect with other spirits, souls, and bodies because we don't love ourselves.

- FINAL THOUGHTS…FINALLY TAKE #3 FINAL THOUGHT

God's heartbeat is for people, and if we connect with the vibration and heartbeat of God then our heartbeat will be for people.

CHAPTER THIRTEEN

BIBLICAL, PROSPEROUS, AND SUCCESSFUL PRAYERS

In the previous chapter we have seen how important it is to communicate and connect with other human beings. In this chapter we will see that the ultimate communication is with the Creator of the universe, God. This is accomplished by prayer. I believe that we must develop a Prayer Paradigm (P.P.)

PRAYER: proseuchē (pros-yoo-khay)'=From G4336; prayer (worship); by implication an oratory (chapel): - X pray earnestly, prayer. G4336: proseuchomai (pros-yoo'-khom-ahee)= to pray to God, that is, supplicate, worship: - pray (X earnestly, for), make prayer.

PARADIGM: (1) a set of forms all of which contain a particular element, especially the set of all inflected forms based on a single stem or theme. (2) A display in fixed arrangement of such a set, as boy's, boys, boys, boys'. (3) An example serving as a model; pattern. (4) A framework containing the basic assumptions, ways of thinking, and methodology that are commonly accepted by members of a scientific community (5) such a cognitive framework shared by members of any discipline or group.

~Dictionary.com

PARADIGM: "Paradigms are a multitude of habits that guide every move you make. They affect the way you eat, the way you walk, even the way you talk. They govern your communication, your work habits, your successes and your failures."

~Bob Proctor

Prayer is the supernatural means of communications to connect with the Creator of the universe. Prayer is not necessarily a monologue where you just pour out your heart to God with your needs and greeds, but it is a dialogue between you and God, because He wants to tell you a few things. The codebook for this communication is 66 books collected in one leather-bound book called the Bible. Harold Hill, who wrote *How to Live like a King's Kid* called the Bible, "The Manufacturer's Handbook."

While you may be prosperous and successful without God, you will never be happy or at peace. You can pull yourself up by your own bootstraps and work your way into what, on the surface, looks like winning and living the *good life,* but the *good life* is a poor substitute for the *abundant life* that Jesus want us to live.

> *"The thief comes but to steal, kill and destroy, but I came that you might have life and that more abundantly."*
>
> ~John 10:10

> *"The thief (the one who tries to enter by another way, another door, religious people and the d-evil) comes only (one reason manifested in three areas) to steal (your desires), kill (your visions) and destroy (your dreams) BUT (in contrast) I (Jesus) came (from heaven to earth for the purpose of destroying the works of the d-evil) that they (you and me) may have life (living), and have it more abundantly (the abundant life)."*
>
> ~John 10:10 with emphasis and additions mine
>
> Ruminator Style

When someone is at war and on the battlefield, one vital thing that must take place is communication with headquarters so they can get directives from a different viewpoint or source. When you are smack dab in the middle of a battle, you are fighting blindly. But when you hear a different perspective you begin to have a *headquarters view* of what is going on and what you need to do. You have what is known as a *bird's eye view* or in our case, a *God's eye view.* Prayer is our connection with headquarters—with heaven—so we can live life out on earth.

NOTE: For 27 years I taught a class at church (Springhouse Worship and Arts Center, originally Smyrna Assembly of God) called The Ruminators Sunday School Class, where I used a whiteboard to diagram the Communication system with God so we could have what is known as "effectual, fervent, prevailing prayer." (James 5:16)

- ## COMMUNICATION HARDWARE

I have touched on these principles throughout this book, but this will be more detail of how we can get instructions from headquarters (God in heaven) to us here on earth. As mentioned previously, the "Communication Codebook" is the Bible.

The main receiver and sender is our human spirit. This is standard hardware. The human spirit, the "lamp of the Lord" (Pro-Verbs 20:27) that in its original state at creation was a clear channel to God with no static on the frequency. When the fall of disobedience took place in the Garden, static entered, and the frequency and vibration with God was skewed. Jesus came to restore the connection with God as we became new creations in Christ. (2 Corinthians 5:17)

Even after we were born again via the cross of Christ (the tower communication) we can still have static on the line because of sin and the god of this world who is the prince of power of air. (2 Corinthians 4:4, Ephesians 2:2) The solution to the static after being born again is the same solution—the cross of Christ which becomes the touchstone of restoration by the blood of Christ which cleanses us from all sin and unrighteousness. (1 John 1:5–10, 1 John 2:1–2) Static on the communication system includes sin, the flesh (carnal nature), rebellion, and transgression. Like our computers, sometimes we need to turn the computer off and restart it. For our spiritual communication this means (1) repentance, having a change of mind, change of heart, change of direction, change of attitude (2) return, to our first love (3) recalibration, getting back on the frequency of God (4) repristination, restoring back to factory settings.

- ## THE WISDOM/MYSTERY COMMUNICATION CONNECTION

God's heartbeat is to speak wisdom to us and that with the wisdom we would have understanding.

> *"Wisdom is the principal thing; therefore get wisdom: and with all thy getting get understanding."*
> ~Pro-Verbs 4:7

> *"The beginning of wisdom is: Get [skillful and godly] wisdom [it is preeminent]! And with all your acquiring, get understanding [actively seek spiritual discernment, mature comprehension, and logical interpretation].*
> ~Pro-Verbs 4:7 AMP

We see that our wisdom is NOT in persuasive words of wisdom, BUT (in contrast) in demonstration (manifestation) of the Spirit (Holy) and power (force, miraculous power, ability abundance, might, strength). (1 Corinthians 2:4)

Why was this demonstration necessary?

> *"So that your faith would not rest on the wisdom of men, but on the power of God."*
> ~1 Corinthians 2:5

In the Word of God, via human beings, wisdom is being spoken about mysteries. It was *hidden wisdom* that is revealed. This revelation is communicated via God.

> *"Yet we do speak wisdom among those who are mature; a wisdom, however, not of this age nor of the rulers of this age, who are passing away; BUT we speak God's wisdom in a mystery, the hidden wisdom which God predestined before the ages to our glory; the wisdom which none of the rulers of this age ha understood; for if they had understood it they would not have crucified the Lord of glory."*
> ~1 Corinthians 2:6–8 emphasis mine

In Isaiah 64:4 and Isaiah 65:17 we see that the mystery is prepared for believers for the purpose of communication that will be explained in 1 Corinthians 2:9–16 where we have *the mind of Christ.*

> *"…things which eye has not seen and ear has not heard and which have not entered the heart of man, ALL THAT GOD HAS PREPARED for those who love Him."*
>
> ~1 Corinthians 2:9 emphasis mine

1. How has God revealed the mystery to us? (1 Corinthians 2:10)

2. What does the Spirit search? (1 Corinthians 2:10)

3. In the Spirit's searching of all things, what does the search include? (1 Corinthians 2:10)

4. What does the Spirit help? (Romans 8:26)

5. What do we NOT know how to do as we should? (Romans 8:26)

6. Who intercedes for us? (Romans 8:26)

7. What is used in this interceding? (Romans 8:26)

8. What are these utterings and groanings considered to be? (Romans 8:26)

NOTE: These uttering and groanings are considered by some to be praying in the Spirit, praying in tongues, a person's prayer language that prays the will of God that the Spirit got while He was in God's presence. I personally pray in this manner and then in English when I am weak, my back is against the wall, and I don't know how to pray about something.

9. What does He who searches the hearts know? (Romans 8:27)

10. What does He do for the saints? (Romans 8:27)

11. What is this intercession for the saints according to? (Romans 8:27)

12. What do we know? (Romans 8:28)

NOTE: God is a causative God who does not cause bad and ugly things but He causes the good, bad and ugly things in our lives to work together synergistically for our good (not bad and ugly).

13. Who does He cause these bad and ugly things to work together for our good for?

a. _____ Romans 8:27
b. _____ Romans 8:28
c. _____ Romans 8:28

NOTE: God's purpose from the beginning (Genesis 3:15) has been to destroy the works of the d-evil. (1 John 3:8) Jesus demonstrated this for three years as He went about doing good and healing all who were harassed and oppressed by the d-evil with the Holy Spirit and power (duNAMis, dynamic miracle ability). (Acts 10:38)

THE PURPOSE:

> *"For those whom He foreknew, He also predestined to become conformed to the image of His Son, so that He would be the first-born among MANY brethren (you and me) and those whom He predestined He also called; these whom He called, He also justified; and these whom He justified, He also glorified."*
> ~Romans 8:29–30 addition and emphasis mine

14. Who among men knows the thoughts of a man? (1 Corinthians 2:11)

15. Where is the spirit (little s) of man located? (1 Corinthians 2:11)

16. Who knows the thoughts of God? (1 Corinthians 2:11, Romans 8:26–27)

17. What have we not received? (1 Corinthians 2:12)

18. What/Who have we received? (1 Corinthians 2:12)

19. Why have we received the Spirit who is from God? (1 Corinthians 2:12)

20. How much does it cost us for this knowledge? (1 Corinthians 2:12)

21. What kind of words was Paul speaking? What kind of words was Paul not speaking? (1 Corinthians 2:13)

22. Who taught the spiritual words? (1 Corinthians 2:13)

23. What was the combination of words taught? (1 Corinthians 2:13)

24. What does the natural man not accept? (1 Corinthians 2:14)

NATURAL: psuchikos (psoo-khee-kos)'=From G5590; sensitive that is, animate (in distinction on the one hand from G4152, which is the higher or renovated nature; and on the other from G5446, which is the lower or bestial nature): - natural, sensual. G5590: psuchē psoo-khay'=From G5594; breath, that is, (by implication) spirit, abstractly or concretely (the animal sentient principle only; thus distinguished on the one hand from G4151, which is the rational and immortal soul; and on the other from G2222, which is mere vitality, even of plants: these terms thus exactly correspond respectively to the Hebrew [H5315], [H7307] and [H2416]: - heart (+ -ily), life, mind, soul, + us, + you. G5594: psuchō=psoo'-kho=A primary verb; to breathe (voluntarily but gently; thus differing on the one hand from G4154, which denotes properly a forcible respiration; and on the other from the base of G109, which refers properly to an inanimate breeze), that is, (by implication of reduction of temperature by evaporation) to chill (figuratively): - wax cold.

NOTE: On one hand you have the spirit, the lamp of the Lord fill with the Holy Spirit and then the natural man, the carnal man, the soulish man without the Holy Spirit. The natural man cannot accept the things of God.

25. What are the things of God to the natural man? (1 Corinthians 2:14)

26. Why can the natural man understand the things of the Spirit? (1 Corinthians 2:14)

NOTE: In the world of business, there are many forms of appraisal. Appraisal of the value and worth of items, the appraisal of business dealings with other human beings, etc. This appraisal will bring various degrees of prosperity and success but most likely it will be void of happiness. But the spiritual man (the human spirit filled with the Holy Spirit) does not find the things of God foolishness and appraises rightly with the cause and effect of having biblical prosperity and success with peace.

27. What does the one who is spiritual do? (1 Corinthians 2:15)

28. Who appraises the spiritual man on an earthly level? (1 Corinthians 2:15)

29. What is needed to know the mind of the Lord? (1 Corinthians 2:16)

30. What do we have? (1 Corinthians 2:16)

• THE MIND OF CHRIST

When we have the *mind of Christ* we think differently on many levels. When we have the mind of Christ we are not just so heavenly minded so that we are no earthly good, but our thought process is enhance, and we are able to see things from a different perspective, from a God's Eyed View (G.E.V.). We think with an Anointed Mind. The mind of Christ is the mind of the Anointed One.

> *"And it shall come to pass in that day, that his burden shall be taken away from off thy shoulder, and his yoke from off thy neck, and the yoke shall be destroyed because of the anointing."*
> ~Isaiah 10:27 KJV

> *"It shall come to pass in that day that his burden will be taken away from your shoulder, and his yoke from your neck, and the yoke will be destroyed because of the anointing oil."*
> ~Isaiah 10:27 NKJV

> *"So it will be in that day, that the burden of the Assyrian will be removed from your shoulders and his yoke from your neck. The yoke will be broken because of the fat."*
> ~Isaiah 10:27 AMP

NOTE: The yoke was the bondage of the Assyrians as they were in captivity. The word destroyed indicates that the yoke will be pulverized to the point of not being usable again. Some theologians indicate that the necks did not shrink in captivity but enlarged to the point of breaking. Others indicate that their necks were oiled and the yoke was unable to withstand the anointing. For us it means God is breaking what holds us in bondage especially being in bondage of the mind, because we have the Anointed mind of The Anointed One.

"As a man thinketh in his heart/mind so he is."
~Pro-Verbs 23:7 KJV with addition mine

"...out of the abundance of the heart the mouth speaks."
~Luke 6:45

NOTE: What we think, with the mind of Christ, the mind of the Anointed One, and His anointing is who we are in Him. When we begin to think with the mind of Christ, we begin to speak the mind/words of Christ, and we begin to do/act in our lives the mind of Christ's anointing in our lives including our business life, our spiritual life, our interpersonal life resulting in prosperity and good success.

"For the mind (natural mind) set on the flesh (carnal nature) is death, but (in contrast) the mind (of Christ, the Anointed on, the anointed mind) set on the Spirit (Holy) is life (and that more abundantly) and peace (wholeness, rest that surpasses all comprehension (what we think)."
~Romans 8:6, Isaiah 10:27, John 10:10, Philippians 4:6–7
addition mine

"You know of Jesus (God is salvation) of Nazareth (here on earth) how God (our Father Who art in heaven) anointed (poured out, smeared on, rubbed into) Him (Jesus the Anointed One) with (the elements) Holy Spirit and power (duNAMis, dynamic ability) and He went about (Matthew 4:23) doing good (not bad) and HEALING ALL (going from the point of being sick to the point of not being sick any longer) who were harassed and oppressed (bad) by the d-evil (not God) for God was with Him (Immanuel God with us)."
~Acts 10 38 with emphasis and additions mine
Ruminator Style

Biblical Prosperity and Success means (1) prosperity=having enough to meet our needs and overflow to help others (2) success=accomplishing the purposes of God.

With the anointed mind of Christ we are able to pray effectual, fervent prayers that line up with the will of God on earth as it is in heaven.

CHAPTER FOURTEEN

PRAYING IN THE SPIRIT
FOR BIBLICAL PROSPERITY AND SUCCESS

In our last chapter we saw the importance of praying with the mind of Christ. We were created with the hardware to connect with God, to get on the same vibration and frequency of God, so we could have a clear channel connection with God with no static.

In this chapter we will look at how to enhance our communication channel with the Creator of the universe. I believe that with a clear channel to the Creator of the universe, creativity will flow to us with creative ideas we can implement in our desires, visions, and dreams with the cause and effect being Biblical Prosperity and Success.

At the end of this chapter we will be studying 1 Corinthians 14 utilizing questions/answers to look at the relationship of tongues in private devotions and in a church service, to keep things all things done *properly/decently and in an orderly manner.* (1 Corinthians 14:40)

I believe that between God and us is a lot of airspace. Our prayers can be hindered due to the d-evil, who is known as "the god of this world." (2 Corinthians 4:4) It appears that the serpent, the d-evil, became the the god of this world when Adam and Eve choose to sin and disobey God's commands which resulted in high treason as they passed on rulership and authority/dominion to the d-evil. (Genesis 3:1–24) The god of this world blinds the eye of people on planet earth so they can't even see the truth. (2 Corinthians 4:1–6) I believe this blindness occurs to believers and non-believers alike and in essence causes static on our line to God disrupting prayers.

- PRAYER WARFARE (Daniel 10:1:1–13)

"Daniel, whose name means "God is my judge", was a statesman in the court of heathen monarchs. Taken captive as a youth to Babylon by Nebuchadnezzar in 605 B.C., he spent the rest of his long life there as a governmental official and as a prophet of the true God (versus their false gods)."
   ~Ryrie Study Bible introduction to the book Daniel

Daniel (aka Belteshazzar) had a revelation—a message was revealed to him. Daniel had been mourning for three entire weeks (21 days). During this time Daniel did not eat any tasty food, meat, or wine. He also did not use ointment (used for anointing/refreshing) for the 21 days. Previously Daniel prayed a prayer of repentance (intercession) for Israel. (Daniel 9:3–19)

"While I was still speaking in prayer then the man Gabriel (a messenger/angel from God in the form of a man) whom I had seen in the vision previous, came to me in my extreme weariness about the time of the evening offering. He gave me instruction and talked with me and said, O Daniel, I have now come forth to give you insight with understanding.
   ~Daniel 9:21 addition mine

(For insight into Gabriel's message read Daniel 9:22–27)
NOTE: Many times we pray and see no result of our communication with God. That does not mean that God has not heard us but that there is a conflict in the heavenly realm.

"Then he (the angel) said to me, Do not be afraid, Daniel for from the first day that you set your heart on understanding this and on humbling yourself before you God, your words (prayers) were heard, and I have come in response to your words (prayers)."
   ~Daniel 10:12 addition mine

NOTE: When you communicate with God, when you say your

prayers, God hears them on the day you prayed them, even if you do not see any visible manifestation or answer. You are praying (walking) by faith and not by sight. (Galatians 5:7)

Why is there a delay in answers to our prayers? I don't know for sure but I do believe that one reason is warfare in the heavenly realm.

> *"But the prince (angels) of the kingdom of Persia (an earthly region) was withstanding (fighting) me for 21 days; then behold, Michael one of the chief princes (angels), came to help me (Gabriel), for I had been left there with the kings of Persia."*
> ~Daniel 10:13 addition mine

NOTE: Daniel communicated with God via prayer. God heard your prayers when you first prayed them. There is angelic warfare by the d-evil's angels (messengers, aka the thorns in the flesh, (2 Corinthians 12:7) to keep you from exalting yourself with answered prayers.

• THE d-evil's SCHEMES

The d-evil is also known as *the prince of the power of the air* (Ephesians 2:2) We pull down the strongholds of the frequency between God by resisting the god of this world and his schemes. (Ephesians 6:10–17) We accomplish this with *"all prayer and petition, pray at all times in the Spirit, and with this in view be on the alert (keep your eyes wide open all the time), with all perseverance (don't give up because the d-evil won't) and petition (specific prayers) for all the saints, and pray for my (Paul's) behalf that utterances (words to speak) may be given to me (in his mind) in the opening of my mouth (speaking) to make known with boldness the mystery of the Gospel (the D.B.R. for the Jews and Gentiles alike)."* (Ephesians 6:18–20, I Peter 5:8–11)

Depending on which part of the theological divide that you are on, this thing called "praying in the Spirit" can be equated with "speaking in tongues" or "speaking in tongues of men or angels" (1 Corinthians13:1) or speaking/praying in your learned natural human language from English to Chinese to Russian to Swahili and beyond.

As a speech-language pathologist who has studied in depth language development and language disorders, I personally believe that praying in the Spirit is both. Believe it or not, God the creator of words and language, is able to understand human beings praying in tongues and human beings praying in a learned language.

The problem some theologians and denominations have with praying in tongues/the Spirit is that it is linked to emotionalism. The term for praying in the Spirit/tongues is glossolalia.

GLOSSOLAIA: incomprehensible speech in an imaginary language, sometimes occurring in a trance state, an episode of religious ecstasy, or schizophrenia.

Some will admit that this thing called *speaking in tongues* or *praying in the Spirit* did occur back in Bible days, but anything connected with the supernatural like tongues/praying in the Spirit, miracles, healings, gifts of the Spirit, etc. ceased happening. The reasons given for this perspective of the ceasing of supernatural events include:

1. The church was established.
2. The last original apostle died.
3. The canon of the Bible (the Word of God) was competed.
4. Any or all of the reasons combined.

These things are considered to be the "perfect" that has come.

Those who believe that the supernatural has ceased usually point to 1 Corinthians 13:8 (After Paul taught the ignorant about active spiritual gifts in 1 Corinthians 12:1–11) as their proof text for the ceasing of especially speaking in tongues.

> "Love never fails; but if there are gifts of prophecy, they will be done away; if there are tongues, they will cease, if there is knowledge, it will be done away. For we know in part and we prophesy in part; but when the perfect comes the partial will be done away."
>
> ~1 Corinthians 12:9–10

NOTE: From that time to the time of this writing, the perfect has not come. In my mind and millions of others "the perfect" is the return of Jesus and not an apostle dying, the completed canon, or even the establishment of the church.

NOTE: I believe to understand the relationship of the supernatural to us today, you must study 1 Corinthians 12, 13, and 14 as one unit. I have written a study called *The Baptism Of/In/With The Holy Spirit (Have You Received Since You Believed)*. It is a verse by verse, fill-in-the-blank study of these chapters.

In 1970 I became a follower of Jesus (a Christian, Born Again, Born Anew, Born From Above).

"Therefore I make know to you that no one speaking by the Spirit of God says, Jesus is accursed; and no one can say Jesus is Lord except by the Holy Spirit."

~1 Corinthians 12:3

In 1970 in I confessed (came into agreement with God) with my mouth Jesus as Lord, and I believed in my heart that God raised Him from the dead, and I was saved. (Romans 10:9) In 1972 I received the baptism of the Holy Spirit with speaking in tongues as I sat in my car, by myself, at 12:00 midnight on the corner of Frisco drive. There was no emotionalism, no crowd of people around me manipulating me with a Pentecostal frenzy. There was "something more" like Catherine Marshall (editor of *Guidepost* magazine, the wife of the chaplain of Congress, Peter Marshall, and author of many books including *Christy, Something More* (about her experience with the Holy Spirit), and *The Helper* (a study of the Holy Spirit). Many people including John Sherrill (*They Speak With Other Tongues*), Pat Boone (*A New Song*), Dennis Bennett, an Episcopal Priest, and his wife, Rita, (*9:00 In The Morning*), and many more famous and anonymous individuals received the Holy Spirit with speaking in tongues subsequent to salvation. It is beyond the scope of this book to go into detail about the subject, but for our purposes I will close out this chapter with a look at praying in tongues and praying in English (or other languages) in relation to individual prayers and in a service. (1 Corinthians chapter 14).

For me as a speech-language pathologist, I believe that praying in the Spirit and in English are necessary for me to walk in Biblical Prosperity and Good Success Ruminator Style. I will be using the question/answer format from 1 Corinthians 14:1–40 and other Scriptures.

The epistle (letter) to the church in Corinth was one of three letters sent to the church (one is missing). Paul is writing a letter of correction to the church, encouraging them to repent and change their behavior. In some incidences he encourages them to cease from their actions, and in others incidences he is telling them not to cease but to correct their behavior and sin. Many like to use these epistles to prove that miracles, healings, gifts of the Spirit have ceased and that those who continue to believe these things are in error, are utilizing poor exegesis (interpretation of the Scriptures), and border on heresy and cult like status.

Actually, the Church of Corinth, also known as the church of God (1 Corinthians 1:2), were continuing on as a Spirit–filled (Pentecostal and Charismatic type) of church. Here are some characteristics of this blowing and going gathering of believers.

a. They were sanctified saints (1 Corinthians 1:2)

b. They were sanctified by Christ Jesus (1 Corinthians 1:2)

c. They were saints by calling (1 Corinthians 1:2)

d. They, like other saints, had called on the name of our Lord Jesus Christ—their Lord and ours (1 Corinthians 1:3)

e. Paul pronounce grace and peace on them

f. Paul thanked God for the church in Corinth for the grace (they didn't deserve it) given them in Christ Jesus. (1 Corinthians 1:4)

g. In everything they were enriched in Him, in all respect and all knowledge (1 Corinthians 1:5)

h. They had a confirmed testimony concerning Christ (1 Corinthians 1:6)

i. They (the church) were not lacking in ANY GIFT (of the Spirit) (1 Corinthians 1:7)

j. They were eagerly awaiting the revelation (the 2nd coming) of our Lord Jesus Christ (1 Corinthians 1:7)

k. The Lord Jesus Christ will confirm them to the end, blameless in the day (when He returns) of our Lord Jesus Christ. (1 Corinthians 1:8)

l. They were called into fellowship with His Son, Jesus Christ, our Lord (1 Corinthians 1:9)

NOTE: This sounds like the type of church that I want to be involved in today. The Church of God in Corinth gets a bad rap. Remember this is a letter of correction and not necessarily a letter of cessation. They were told to cease fleshly, carnal habits and the abuse of the gifts but not the spiritual gifts in their lives.

NOTE: Word about their bad behavior had got around to Paul, thus the reason for the letter.

a. There were divisions in the church (1 Corinthians 1:10)

b. There were quarrels among them (1 Corinthians 1:10)

c. There were arguments over who was the superior teacher, Apollos, Paul, Cephas (Peter), and some played the Christ card, that they only listened to Jesus (on the surface it looks good but even that was divisive) (1 Corinthians 1:11–12)

d. There were issues about whose name they were baptized in to the point that Paul was thanking God that he did not baptize any of them except a couple. Paul could not remember those who he baptized except of a couple. (1 Corinthians 1: 13–17)

NOTE: I find it interesting that Christ did not send Paul to baptize people but to preach the Gospel, the D.B.R. (1 Corinthians 15:1–5) not in cleverness of speech so that the CROSS OF CHRIST would not be made void. (1 Corinthians 1:17)

e. They were in the flesh (carnal nature) with jealously and strife among them (1 Corinthians 3:1–3)

f. They were elevating teachers above each other. (1 Corinthians 3:4–9)

g. There was immorality in the church (there is nothing new under the sun). Including a man having sex with his father's wife (incest) (1 Corinthians 5:1)

h. Arrogance and no repentance or sorrow because of these immoral sins. (1 Corinthians 5:2)

i. They associated with the immoral persons, the covetous, the idolater, the swindler, the reviler, the drunkard. (1 Corinthians 5:11–13)

NOTE: At this point there is no mention of speaking in tongues, prophecy etc. We will cover that in our next section.

j. They were suing one another in heathen courts. (1 Corinthians 6:1–8)

k. There was moral laxity as evidenced by: fornicators, idolaters, adulterers, effeminate, homosexuals, thieves, covetous, drunkards, revilers, swindlers. (1 Corinthians 6:9–20)

l. There were issues in marriage and celibacy (1 Corinthians 7:1–40)

k. There was issues with offerings to idols (1 Corinthians 8:1–13)

NOTE: The same issues that the fathers had in the wilderness were the same issues that were in the church of Corinth and served as an example for them and us so we will not be laid low in the wilderness including:

(1) Don't crave evil things

(2) Don't be idolaters

(3) Don't act immorally

(4) Don't try/test the Lord

(5) Don't grumble and complain

(6) Don't think that you are standing because you will fall.

All of these things happened to the children of Israel in the wilderness, was happening to the church in Corinth, and can happen to us.

m. They were taking the Lord's Supper in an unworthy manner (unworthily) by greedily eating all the food, drinking all the wine, getting drunk before anyone else was able to partake, and eating things offered to idols (1 Corinthians 10:14–33, 1 Corinthians 11:17–34)

o. There were issues of public worship by men and women. (1 Corinthians 11:1–15)

NOTE: No, the church in Corinth was not perfect, but neither are we. Some things were to cease, like sexual immorality, while other things were not to cease but be corrected, like abuse of the gifts of the Spirit.

Now, let's look at the private gifts and the public gifts corrections utilizing a question/answer format.

1. What are we to pursue? (1 Corinthians 14:1)

2. Out of faith, hope, and love what is the greatest? (1 Corinthians 13:13)

NOTE: This does not mean that faith and hope are inferior, but love is the motivator. Faith works by love and hope (confident expectation) is for things hoped for by faith. (Hebrews 11:1)

3. While we are in pursuit of love, what are we to yet desire? (1 Corinthians 14:1)

NOTE: Apparently, in 55 A.D. after the crucifixion of Jesus, the coming of the Holy Spirit, and the establishment of the church the need for spiritual gifts was still in vogue. They were instructed to not only desire spiritual gifts but to earnestly desire them.

EARNESTLY DESIRE: zēloō (dzay-lo'-o)=From G2205; to have warmth of feeling for or against: - affect, covet (earnestly), (have) desire, (move with) envy, be jealous over, (be) zealous (-ly affect). G2205: zēlos (dzay'-los)=From G2204; properly heat, that is, (figuratively) "zeal" (in a favorable sense, ardor; in an unfavorable one, jealousy, as of a husband [figuratively of God], or an enemy, malice): - emulation, envy (-ing), fervent mind, indignation, jealousy, zeal. G2204: zeō (dzeh'-o)=A primary verb; to be hot (boil, of liquids; or glow, of solids), that is, (figuratively) be fervid (earnest): - be fervent.

4. When someone speaks in a tongue, who are they *not* speaking to? (1 Corinthians 14:2)

5. When someone is speaking in a tongue, who *are* they speaking to? (1 Corinthians 14:2)

6. When someone speaks in a tongue, who understands? (1 Corinthians 14:2)

7. From what location is someone who speaks in a tongue, speaking from? (1 Corinthians 14:2)

8. What is someone speaking in tongues, speaking from his spirit (little s, the lamp of the Lord, the third part of the trinity of man (1 Corinthians 14:2, I Thessalonians 5:23, Pro-Verbs 20:27), what are they speaking? (1 Corinthians 14:2)

9. Who is the one who prophesies speaking to? (1 Corinthians 14:3)

10. What three things happens when a person prophesies? (1 Corinthians 14:3)

    a. _____

b. _____

c. _____

10. What happens when one speaks in a tongue? (1 Corinthians 14:4)

NOTE: Edification of self when you speak in a tongue is NOT a bad thing. It is not a matter of pride but one of humility.

11. Who does one who prophesies edify? (1 Corinthians 14:4)

12. What did Paul wish everyone did? (1 Corinthians 14:5)

NOTE: It does not look like Paul is trying to get everyone to cease practicing speaking in tongues, whether to themselves of to the church.

13. What did Paul wish everyone did more than speak in tongues? (1 Corinthians 14:5)

14. Who is greater, the prophesier or the tongue talker? (1 Corinthians 14:5)

15. What is the rule of exception about who is greater? (1 Corinthians 14:5)

NOTE: One of the gifts of the Spirit found in 1 Corinthians 12:1:8–10, is the interpretation of tongues.

16. Why is the interpretation of tongues so important for the church? (1 Corinthians 14:5)

17. There will be no profit for you if I come speaking to you in tongues unless four things takes place. What are those four things? (1 Corinthians 14:6)

a. _____

b. _____

c. _____

d. _____

18. Lifeless things produce sound but what do they need to produce? (1 Corinthians 14:7)

19. What will not be if there is not a distinction of tones? (1 Corinthians 14:7)

20. What will happen if a bugle produces an indistinct sound versus a distinct sound? (1 Corinthians 14:8)

21. In comparison to a musical instrument (the bugle), what must you utter by the tongue? (1 Corinthians 14:9)

22. What is the cause and effect of uttering a tongue with clear speech? (1 Corinthians 14:9)

23. If you utter unclear speech, what will you be doing? (1 Corinthians 14:9)

NOTE: At this point we see that there was a misuse of this thing called speaking in tongues, but at this point there is no instruction to stop speaking in tongues.

24. What are there in the world? (1 Corinthians 14:10)

NOTE: There are currently 7,102 languages in the world, where people speak in different human tongues and dialects. Can you imagine the chaos and confusion if someone preached in a language with no interpretation in the natural? Think about the confusion in a service if various people were speaking in tongues over one another with no interpretation. There would be chaos and confusions.

NOTE TO THE NOTE: I believe that as we continue our study we will see a difference between speaking in a tongue in a church service versus praying in tongues, in the spirit, in our prayer life.

25. What do the 7,102 various languages in the world have in common? (1 Corinthians 14:10)

26. What will you be if you do not know the meaning of the language, and what will you be to the one who speaks? (1 Corinthians 14:11)

27. What were the Corinthians considered to be in their zeal of spiritual gifts (of the Holy Spirit? (1 Corinthians 14:11–12)

28. What should they seek and why should they see this? (1 Corinthians 14:12)

NOTE: The next verse start with the word *therefore*, which means we should see what the next statement is "there for" based on the previous statement.

29. What should the one who speaks in a tongue (in a church service) pray for? (1 Corinthians 14:13)

30. What/who is praying when you pray in a tongue? (1 Corinthians 14:13, Pro-Verbs 20:27)

31. What is the mind? (1 Corinthians 14:13)

NOTE: Remember that you are a spirit, and you have a mind that is in a body. (1 Corinthians 5:23) When your spirit is praying in tongues, your mind is unfruitful—and so is the mind of those who hear you, unless there is an interpretation of the tongue. Speaking in tongues plus an interpretation equals prophecy.

32. When you pray with the spirit (little s), what will you pray with also? (1 Corinthians 14:15)

33. When you sing with the spirit (little s), what will you sing with also? (1 Corinthians 14:15)

34. If you bless in the spirit only, how will the one who fills the place (the church) of the ungifted say what? (1 Corinthians 14:16)

35. What are you giving when you pray in tongues/the Spirit? (1 Corinthians 14:17)

36. What is the person NOT being at your giving of thanks? (1 Corinthians 14:17)

37. What did Paul thank God for? (1 Corinthians 14:18)

38. Who did Paul speak in tongues more than? (1 Corinthians 14:18)

39. When Paul was in the church what did He want to do? (1 Corinthians 14:19)

40. Why did Paul want to speak five words with his mind? (1 Corinthians 14:19)

NOTE: The ratio of speaking in tongues and speaking words with the mind was 5/10,000 words. The reason is edification, building up the others in the church. Apparently, the goal of this letter of correction was NOT cessation of the gifts of the Spirit but to continue in the gifts, but do it properly.

41. What were they to be in their thinking? (1 Corinthians 14:20)

42. What was written in the Law? (Isaiah 14:21, 1 Corinthians 14:21)

43. Who are tongues *not* a sign for? (1 Corinthians 14:22)

44. Who *are* tongues a sign for? (1 Corinthians 14:22)

45. Who is prophecy *not* for? (1 Corinthians 14:22)

46. Who *is* prophecy for? (1 Corinthians 14:22)

47. What if the whole church assembles together and all speak in tongues and then the ungifted men or unbelievers enter, what will they say? (1 Corinthians 14:23)

48. What if all prophesy (instead of all speaking in tongues) and an unbeliever or ungifted person enters (the church/gathering) what is the cause and effect of the prophetic? (1 Corinthians 14:24)

a. _____

b. _____

49. What will be disclosed? (1 Corinthians 14:24)

50. What will the unbeliever and ungifted man do when prophecy is given? (1 Corinthians 14:25)

NOTE: In many denominations and theological seminaries, prophecy is equated with just natural preaching while tongues is equated with pseudo-supernatural gibberish. I see a combination of both minus the gibberish element. In 1 Corinthians 12:10 prophecy is lumped in with tongues and the interpretation of tongues along with the other gifts of the Spirit.

"But one and the same Spirit (Holy) works all these things, distributing to each one individually as He (the Holy Spirit) wills."
                                    ~1 Corinthians 14:11 addition mine

In 1 Corinthians 14:26–40 Paul lays out the regulations for the use of the gifts and not the cessation of the gifts of the Spirit within a gathering of saints and sinners.

51. What is the outcome when the brethren (and sistern) assemble? (1 Corinthians 14:26)

a. _____

b. _____

c. _____

d. _____

e. _____

52. Why are all of these things done? (1 Corinthians 14:26)

"If anyone speaks in a tongue, it should be by two or at the most three, and each in turn, and one must interpret; but if there is no interpreter he must keep silent in the church and let him speak to himself and to God."
                                    ~1 Corinthians 14:27

NOTE: The correction is that everyone should not be speaking at once and over one another causing confusion, and then there must be an interpretation. If no one is there to interpret, then be quiet and do not continue with the chaos and confusion. There is no edification in chaotic and confusing behavior.

NOTE TO THE NOTE: We have established early on that they should desire earnestly spiritual gifts including tongues, interpretation, and prophecy. In 1 Corinthians 14:27 if there is no interpretation of the tongues (which equals prophecy that speak and edifies men) then let him speak to himself and God and edify himself. (1 Corinthians 14:28) (1 Corinthians 14:1–4)

"Let (allow it) all things be done for edification (building up)."
~1 Corinthians 14:26 addition mine

NOTE TO THE NOTE TO THE NOTE: Edifying yourself is not a bad thing. It is a good thing as you talk to yourself in your private prayer language and God.

"But ye, beloved, building up yourselves on your most holy faith, praying in the Holy Ghost, Keep yourselves in the love of God, looking for the mercy of our Lord Jesus Christ unto eternal life."
~Jude 1:20–21 KJV

"But you, beloved, building yourselves up on your most holy faith, praying in the Holy Spirit, keep yourselves in the love of God, looking forward to the mercy of our Lord Jesus Christ to eternal life."
~Jude 1:20–21 NASB

"But you, beloved, build yourselves up on [the foundation of] your most holy faith [continually progress, rise like an edifice higher and higher], pray in the Holy Spirit, and keep yourselves in the love of God, waiting anxiously and looking forward to the mercy of our Lord Jesus Christ [which will bring you] to eternal life."
~Jude 1:20–21 AMP

Paul also taught that part of the spiritual warfare tactics to stand against the schemes of the d-evil is prayer. After putting on the whole armor of God (Ephesians 6:10–17) he encourages prayer.

> *"With all prayer and petition pray at all times in the Spirit, and with this in vie, be on the alert with all perseverance and petition for all the saints and pray on my (Paul's) behalf that utterance may be given to me in the opening of my mouth to make known with boldness the mystery of the gospel (D.B.R., 1 Corinthians 15:1–5) for which I am an ambassador (2 Corinthians 5:18–20) in chains, that in proclaiming it I may speak boldly as I ought to speak."*
> ~Ephesians 6:18–20 addition mine

We see in 1 Corinthians 14:33 that *"...God is not a God of confusion but of peace..."* For the church of God in Corinth, among the others sins and corrections pointed out by Paul, there was the issue of misuse of the gifts of the spirit with rampant disregard for one another as they were speaking in tongues. People were prophesying but there were multiple prophesies and multiple tongues and multiple interpretations. Combine that with women who were on one side of the room trying to communicate with the men on the other side of the room. This was not necessarily an issue of women can't be spiritual, but it was disruptive to the meeting, so Paul urged the women be quiet and quit causing confusion.

"If anyone (man or woman) thinks he is a prophet or spiritual, let him recognize that the things which I wrote to you (in the letter of correction) are the Lord's commandment." If they did not recognize that it is from God, they would not be recognized.

Many use 1 Corinthians 14 at their proof text that tongues are forbidden, and they have ceased having purpose and function.

> *"Therefore, my brethren desire earnestly to prophesy and DO NOT FORBID TO SPEAK IN TONGUES. (In bold and large letters on purpose) But (in contrast to forbidding to speak in tongues) all things must be done properly and in an orderly manner."*
> ~1 Corinthians 14:29–30 additiona and emphasis mine

I believe the lesson learned is that whether you are in a corporate business meeting or in a church service, for prosperity and success, things must be decent and in order.

NOTE: I believe that believers in Christ who have never spoken in tongues in a service or in their private prayer life are born again, love the Lord with all of their hearts, souls, minds, and strength and they love their neighbors as themselves, can pray effectively to God, can have the fruit of the Spirit growing and manifesting in their lives, and yes, can move in the gifts of the Spirit. However for me, I see the necessity of praying in the Spirit (in tongues) in my private prayer life as the Holy Spirit that dwells in my human spirit (the lamp of the Lord) who also is in the presence of God, know the will of God and prays through me with utterings and groanings that I can't understand, and is praying the perfect will of God when I don't know how to pray.

I like what David Wilkerson (author of the *Cross and the Switchblade* and founder of Teen Challenge (a drug rehabilitation organization) in New York City, New York and international) said; "I would rather work with a turned-on Baptist who never spoke in tongues than a cold Pentecostal, any day."

I also believe that I can not only pray and sing in the Spirit, but I can also pray with understanding and my mind more effectively. For me, the cause and effect is I can see provision in my life that I will always have enough to meet my needs and an overflow to help others, and that I will accomplish the purposes of God in my life—that is Biblical Prosperity and Success Ruminator Style.

CHAPTER FIFTEEN

GOD'S PRO-VISION

NOTE: As we come to the end of the book on Biblical Prosperity and Success, I thought that we would review various Scriptures and principles/laws that deal with God's heartbeat for His Pro-Vision for us and for others through us. Take your time, look up the verses, fill in the blanks, and as you do, ask the Holy Spirit to teach you and then begin to apply the various principles/laws.

"Where there is no vision, the people perish: but he that keepeth the law, happy is he."
~Pro-Verbs 29:18 KJV

"Where there is no vision, the people are unrestrained, But happy is one who keeps the Law."
~Pro-Verbs 29:18 NASB

"Where there is no vision [no revelation of God and His word], the people are unrestrained; But happy and blessed is he who keeps the law [of God]."
Pro-Verbs 29:18 AMP

I love to take the word Proverbs and separate the word "Pro" and the word "Verb" making it Pro-Verbs, Positive-Action words. The book of Pro-Verbs is a book of Positive Actions on how to live your life.

In the same way, the word *provision* can be made "Pro-Vision" or Positive Insights into God meeting your every need, spiritually, emotionally and financially. The key to prosperity and success is being able to see that God is the revealer of your provision.

In the Old Testament, one of the compound names of the Lord is Jehovah-Jireh. People teach and even sings songs about how Jehovah Jireh's grace is sufficient. It is my understanding that Jehovah-Jireh literally means, "The revealer of the provision." Yes, He most definitely is our provider, but to know the provision you have to see it, and God will reveal to us where it is located. In Genesis 22:1–19 Abraham was about to sacrifice his son Isaac to the Lord. When Isaac questioned where the sacrifice was, his father told him, "God will provide for himself a lamb." (Genesis 22:8) With his knife raised above his son, the angle of the Lord stopped him, and then the ram was reveled in the thicket. (Genesis 22:13) God not only provided the provision of a sacrifice, God revealed where the sacrifice was. The place was named, Jehovah-Jireh, the Lord the provider, or Yahweh-Yireh (Jehovah Jireh), "the Lord will see to it." The bottom line is that God was the God of Pro-Vision then, and God is the God of Pro-Vision now.

I am dwelling now on the different incidences of the God of Pro-Vision giving and the ways that He gives and provides for our needs. God is not limited to one way of Pro-Vision or one method of providing. God is not bound by the impossibilities of life. There are a multiplicity of possibilities just like there are a multiplicity of colors within the color spectrum or the multiplicity of seeds and harvests in the field of this life or the multiplicityof nerves and brain cells that are found within the crown of His creation, human beings. It is a truth that the only limits that we place on ourselves are our unbelief, our fears, and our doubts.

- GOD'S FAVOR (Pro-Verbs 3:4)

"So you will find favor and good repute in the sight of God and man."

~Pro-Verbs 3:4

FAVOR: chên (khane)=From H2603; graciousness, that is,

subjectively (kindness, favor) or objectively (beauty): - favour, grace (-ious), pleasant, precious, [well-] favoured. H2603: chânan(khaw-nan')= A primitive root (compare H2583); properly to bend or stoop in kindness to an inferior; to favor, bestow; causatively to implore (that is, move to favor by petition): - beseech, X fair, (be, find, shew) favour (-able), be (deal, give, grant (gracious (-ly), intreat, (be) merciful, have (shew) mercy (on, upon), have pity upon, pray, make supplication, X very.

GOOD: tôb (tobe)=From H2895; good (as an adjective) in the widest sense; used likewise as a noun, both in the masculine and the feminine, the singular and the plural (good, a good or good thing, a good man or woman; the good, goods or good things, good men or women), also as an adverb (well): - beautiful, best, better, bountiful, cheerful, at ease, X fair (word), (be in) favour, fine, glad, good (deed, -lier, liest, -ly, -ness, -s), graciously, joyful, kindly, kindness, liketh (best), loving, merry, X most, pleasant, + pleaseth, pleasure, precious, prosperity, ready, sweet, wealth, welfare, (be) well ([-favoured]). H2895: tôb (tobe)-A primitive root, to be (transitively do or make) good (or well) in the widest sense: - be (do) better, cheer, be (do, seem) good, (make), goodly, X please, (be, do, go, play) well.

REPUTE:ekel śêkel (seh'-kel, say'-kel)=From H7919; intelligence; by implication success: - discretion, knowledge, policy, prudence, sense, understanding, wisdom, wise H7919: śâkal (saw-kal')=A primitive root; to be (causatively make or act) circumspect and hence intelligent: - consider, expert, instruct, prosper, (deal) prudent (-ly), (give) skill (-ful), have good success, teach, (have, make to) understand (-ing), wisdom, (be, behave self, consider, make) wise (-ly), guide wittingly.

1. What two things will we receive? (Pro-Verbs 3:4)
2. In whose sight will we receive favor and good repute from? (Pro-Verbs 3:4)
3. What should we not forget? (Pro-Verbs 3:1)
4. What should we allow our hearts to do? (Pro-Verbs 3:1)

5. If we don't forget our Heavenly Father's teachings and keep His commandments, what are three benefits for us? (Pro-Verbs 3:1–2)

6. What are we to do with the Father's teachings and commandments? (Pro-Verbs 1:3)

7. What two thing will we find? (See # 1)

NOTE: As we walk among other human beings, because we have favor and good repute (understanding) with God, we can expect favor with other human beings.

8. What are we to do with all our hearts? (Pro-Verbs 3:5)

9. What are we NOT to lean on? (Pro-Verbs 3:5)

10. What are we to do with all of our ways? (Pro-Verbs 3:6)

11. What will God do when you trust in the Lord with all of your heart, and not lean on your own understanding? (Pro-Verbs 3:6)

12. What are we not to be in our own eyes? (Pro-Verbs 3:7)

13. Who are we to fear? (Pro-Verbs 3:7)

"Wherefore, my beloved, as ye have always obeyed, not as in my presence only, but now much more in my absence, work out your own salvation with fear and trembling."
~Philippians 2:12 KJV

NOTE: Jesus told us to "fear not." Fear negates our faith in God, and we submit to the Lordship of fear. We are told that perfect love casts out all fear.

"There is no fear in love; but perfect love casts out fear: because fear hath torment. He that fears is not made perfect in love."
~1 John 4:18 KJV

NOTE TO THE NOTE: It appears that 1 John 4:18 and Philippian 2:12 are contradictions, but they are not. One fear is filled with doubt and unbelief given by the d-evil and the other is a healthy respect to God who is in control.

14. What will it be if you are not wise in your own eyes, fear the Lord and turn from evil? (Pro-Verbs 3:8)

15. What are we to do with our wealth (that God gave us the

power to make) and from the first (fruits) of all of your produce (aka the tithe, 10%)? (Pro-Verbs 3:9, Deuteronomy 8:18)

16. What will the cause and effect be of honoring the Lord from our wealth and from the first of all of our produce? (Pro-Verbs 3:10)

a._____

b._____

- SPIRITUAL BLESSINGS (Ephesians 1:13)

"Blessed be the God and Father of our Lord Jesus Christ, who has blessed us with every spiritual blessing in the heavenly places in Christ."

~Ephesians 1:13

BLESSED: eulogētos (yoo-log-ay-tos')=From G2127; adorable: - blessed. G2127: eulogeō (yoo-log-eh'-o)=; to speak well of, that is, (religiously) to bless (thank or invoke a benediction upon, prosper): - bless, praise.

BLESSINGS: eulogia (yoo-log-ee'-ah)=From the same as G2127; fine speaking, that is, elegance of language; commendation ("eulogy"), that is, (reverentially) adoration; religiously, benediction; by implication consecration; by extension benefit or largess: - blessing (a matter of) bounty (X -tifully), fair speech. G2127: eulogeō (yoo-log-eh'-op)=to speak well of, that is, (religiously) to bless (thank or invoke a benediction upon, prosper): - bless, praise.

1. Who is blessed? (Ephesians 1:3)
2. Who is God the Father of? (Ephesians 1:3)
NOTE: Lord (kurios, Sir, Master, the controller) Jesus (God is salvation) The Christ (the Anointed One).
3. Who is the one who blesses us? (Ephesians 1:3)
4. What has God the Father blessed us with? (Ephesians 1:3)
NOTE: There is no limit to His blessings for us.
5. What place are these spiritual blessings found? (Romans 1:3)

6. Where are these blessings found in the heavenly? (Romans 1:3)

• THE PERFECT GIFTS (James 1:17)

"Every good thing given and every perfect gift is from above, coming down from the Father of lights, with whom there is no variation of shifting shadow"

~James 1:17

NOTE: James 1:16 indicates that people can be deceived about good things and gifts. Sometimes people think that they either gave themselves the gifts or even that the d-evil is the giver. DO... NOT...BE...DECEIVED!

1. What kind of things are given? (James 1:17)

2. Where does every good thing and every perfect gift come from? (James 1:17)

NOTE: Above instead of below. Above=Heaven. Below=hell. Below heaven can also mean Planet Earth, where humans are the givers!

3. How is the giver of good things and perfect lights described? James 1:17)

4. What is there not with the Father of lights? (James 1:17)

NOTE: Usually, when there is light, there are shadows, but not in the perfect light. Shadows are cast by things on the earth.

5. What is God? (1 John 1:5)

6. What is there not in God? (1 John 1:5)

7. What do we not have when we walk in the darkness? (1 John 1:6)

8. When we lie, what do we not practice? (1 John 1:6)

9. How can we have fellowship (sharing life)? (1 John 1:7)

10. How can we be cleansed from all sin? (1 John 1:7)

NOTE: Sin is darkness, and the only way to ignite the lamp in our lives is by the blood of Jesus, God's Son, who cleanses us from all sin.

11. What was in The Word/Jesus? (John 1:4)

12. What was life? (John 1:4)

13. Where does the Light shine? (John 1:4)

14. What did the darkness not comprehend? (John 1:5)

15. What did the true Light who came into the world do? (John 1:9)

NOTE: The ultimate perfect Light that came from above, from the Father of Lights was Jesus, the Word.

16. Who did The Light say were the lights in the world? (Matthew 5:14)

17. What were the lights (you and me) supposed to allow? (Matthew 5:16)

18. In what way will people in the darkness see the light shine? (Matthew 5:16)

19. When human beings allow the light (from within) to shine in the dark world, Who gets glorified? Where is He? (Matthew 5:16)

- ## THE BENEFITS PACKAGE WITH BLESSINGS FLOWING (Psalm 103:1-5)

"Bless the Lord, O my soul and forget none of His benefits."
~Psalm 103:2

NOTE: In God's Kingdom, we have a benefits package. We access the benefits of God by faith and by blessing the Lord.

BENEFITS: gemûl (ghem-ool')=From H1580; treatment, that is, an act (of good or ill); by implication service or requital: - + as hast served, benefit, desert, deserving, that which he hath given, recompence, reward. H1580: gâmal (gaw-mal')=A primitive root; to treat a person (well or ill), that is, benefit or requite; by implication (of toil) to ripen, that is, (specifically) to wean: - bestow on, deal bountifully, do (good), recompense, requite, reward, ripen, + serve, wean, yield.

1. What do we command to bless the Lord? (Psalm 103:1-2)

SOUL (Hebrew) nephesh (neh'-fesh)=From H5314; properly a breathing creature, that is, animal or (abstractly) vitality; used very widely in a literal, accommodated or figurative sense (bodily or mental): - any, appetite, beast, body, breath, creature, X dead (-ly), desire, X [dis-] contented, X fish, ghost, + greedy, he, heart (-y), (hath,

X jeopardy of) life (X in jeopardy), lust, man, me, mind, mortality, one, own, person, pleasure, (her-, him-, my-, thy-) self, them (your) -selves, + slay, soul, + tablet, they, thing, (X she) will, X would have it. H5314: nâphash (naw-fash')=A primitive root; to breathe; passively, to be breathed upon, that is, (figuratively) refreshed (as if by a current of air): - (be) refresh selves (-ed).

SOUL (Greek) psuchē (psoo-khay')=From G5594; breath, that is, (by implication) spirit, abstractly or concretely (the animal sentient principle only; thus distinguished on the one hand from G4151, which is the rational and immortal soul; and on the other from G2222, which is mere vitality, even of plants: these terms thus exactly correspond respectively to the Hebrew [H5315], [H7307] and [H2416]: - heart (+ -ily), life, mind, soul, + us, + you. G5594: psuchō

(psoo'-kho)=A primary verb; to breathe (voluntarily but gently; thus differing on the one hand from G4154, which denotes properly a forcible respiration; and on the other from the base of G109, which refers properly to an inanimate breeze), that is, (by implication of reduction of temperature by evaporation) to chill (figuratively): - wax cold.

NOTE: Both words in the Hebrew and the Greek indicate a breath. We speak thoughts, words by our breath, frequencies, and vibrations. So it is when we speak God's thoughts and God's Words, by our human breath, but it is by the breath of the Holy Spirit that makes God's super manifest in our natural.

NOTE: Between Psalm 103:3-5 there are six benefits listed (not all the benefits of God).

BENEFIT # 1: What does God pardon and how many of them? (Psalm 103:3)

BENEFIT # 2: What does God do with ALL of our dis-eases? (Psalm 103:3)

BENEFIT # 3: What does God redeem (buy back) our lives from? (Psalm 103:4)

BENEFIT # 4: What does God crown us with? (Psalm 103:4)

BENEFIT # 5: What does God satisfy our years with? (Psalm 103:5)

BENEFIT # 6: What is the cause and effect of our years being satisfied with good things? (Psalm 103:5)

NOTE: As I review our benefits package I believe that this is the abundant life that Jesus promised (John 10:10)

- EXCEEDING BLESSINGS (Ephesians 3:14-20)

"Now to Him who is able to do far more ABUNDANTLY… BEYOND…ALL that we ASK or THINK, according to (based on) the POWER (dunamis, dynamic, miracle ability) that WORKS within us."

~Ephesians 3:20 emphasis and addition mine

NOTE: Ephesians 3:20 is rooted back to Ephesians 3:1-13, the mystery revealed (that the Gentiles are fellow heirs and fellow members of the body (of Christ and fellow partakers of the PROMISE in Christ Jesus through the Gospel/Good News of the Death, Burial, Resurrection of Jesus. (1 Corinthians 15:1-5)

1. What did Paul pray that the church (you and me) would be granted based on the riches of His glory? (Ephesians 3:16-19)

a._____

b. _____

c._____

d. _____

e._____

f. _____

STRENGTHEN: krataioō (krat-ah-yo'-o)=From G2900; to empower, that is, (passively) increase in vigor: - be strenghtened, be (wax) strong. G2900: krataios (krat-ah-yos')=From G2904; powerful: - mighty.G2904: kratos (krat'-os)=Perhaps a primary word; vigor ["great"], (literally or figuratively): - dominion, might [-ily], power, strength.

CHRIST: Christos (khris-tos')=From G5548; anointed, that is, the Messiah, an epithet of Jesus: - Christ. G5548: chriō (khree'-o)=Probably akin to G5530 through the idea of contact; to smear or rub with oil, that is, (by implication) to consecrate to an office or religious service: - anoint.

NOTE: When Christ, The Anointed One, is dwelling in your hearts, His anointing is there also, and He was anointed with yoke breaking, burden lifting, oppression and harassment removing, healing dynamic ability of the Holy Ghost, because God was with Him (Immanuel God with us). (Acts 10:38, Matthew 1:23, Isaiah 7:14, Isaiah 10:27)

DWELL: katoikeō (kat-oy-keh'-o)= to house permanently, that is, reside (literally or figuratively): - dwell (-er), inhabitant (-ter).

ROOTED: rhizoō (hrid-zo'-o)=From G4491; to root (figuratively become stable): - root. G4491: rhiza (hrid'-zah)=Apparently a primary word; a "root" (literally or figuratively): - root.

GROUNDED: themelioō (them-el-ee-o'-o)=From G2310; to lay a basis for, that is, (literally) erect, or (figuratively) consolidate: - (lay the) found (-ation), ground, settle. G2310: themelios (them-el'-ee-os)=; something put down, that is, a substruction (of a building, etc.), (literally or figuratively): - foundation.

LOVE: agapē (ag-ah'-pay)=From G25; love, that is, affection or benevolence; specifically (plural) a love feast: - (feast of) charity ([-ably]), dear, love. G25: agapaō (ag-ap-ah'-o)=Perhaps from ἄγαν agan (much; or compare [H5689]); to love (in a social or moral sense): - (be-) love (-ed).

COMPRHEND: katalambanō (kat-al-am-ban'-o= to take eagerly, that is, seize, possess, etc. (literally or figuratively): - apprehend, attain, come upon, comprehend, find, obtain, perceive, (over-) take.

KNOW: ginōskō (ghin-oce'-ko)=A prolonged form of a primary

verb; to "know" (absolutely), in a great variety of applications and with many implications (as shown at left, with others not thus clearly expressed): - allow, be aware (of), feel, (have) known (-ledge), perceive, be resolved, can speak, be sure, understand.

FILLED UP: plēroō (play-ro'-o)=From G4134; to make replete, that is, (literally) to cram (a net), level up (a hollow), or (figuratively) to furnish (or imbue, diffuse, influence), satisfy, execute (an office), finish (a period or task), verify (or coincide with a prediction), etc.: - accomplish, X after, (be) complete, end, expire, fill (up), fulfil, (be, make) full (come), fully preach, perfect, supply. G4134: plēthō (play'-tho, pleh'-o,)=A prolonged form of a primary word πλέω pleō (which appears only as an alternate in certain tenses and in the reduplicated form of πίμπλημι pimplēmi to "fill" (literally or figuratively [imbue, influence, supply]); specifically to fulfil (time): - accomplish, full (. . . come), furnish.

2. What will we strengthened with? (Ephesians 3:16)

3. Where will this strengthening take place? (Ephesian 3:16)

4. Who will this strengthening be through? (Ephesians 3:16)

3. Where will Christ dwell and how will this happen? (Ephesians 3:17)

4. What will you be rooted and grounded in? (Ephesians 3:17)

5. What will we be able to comprehend with all the saints? (Ephesians 3:18)

a._____

b. _____

c._____

d. _____

6. What will we know? (Ephesians 3:19)

7. What does this knowledge of love surpass? (Ephesians 3:19)

8. What is the purpose of this surpassing knowledge of the love of Christ for? (Ephesians 3:19)

9. What is HE (God the Father) able to do far more abundantly beyond? (Ephesians 3:20)

10. What is this according to? (Ephesians 3:20)

11. Where does this power work? (Ephesians 3:20)

• THE NEED MEETER (Philippians 4:19)

"And my God will supply all your needs according to His riches in glory in Christ Jesus."
~Philippians 4:19

"And my God will liberally supply (fill to the full) your every need according to His riches in glory in Christ Jesus."
~Philippians 4:19 AMP

"And God will/shall ALL of Rodney Lewis Boyd's (put your name in place of mine) needs (not my greed) according to (based on) His (God's) riches (wealth (as fulness), that is, (literally) money, possessions, or (figuratively) abundance, richness, (specifically) valuable bestowment: - riches) in glory (in His presence by praise and worship) in Christ (the Anointed One and His anointing) Jesus (His only unique Son)."
~Philippians 4:19 additions and emphasis mine
Ruminator Style

1. Who is the supplier of your needs? (Philippians 4:19)

SUPPLY: plēroō (play-ro'-o)=From G4134; to make replete, that is, (literally) to cram (a net), level up (a hollow), or (figuratively) to furnish (or imbue, diffuse, influence), satisfy, execute (an office), finish (a period or task), verify (or coincide with a prediction), etc.: - accomplish, X after, (be) complete, end, expire, fill (up), fulfil, (be, make) full (come), fully preach, perfect, supply. G4134: plērēs (play'-race)=From G4130; replete, or covered over; by analogy complete: - full. G4130: plērēs (play'-race)= plēthō (play'-tho, pleh'-o), A prolonged form of a primary word πλέω pleō (which appears only as an alternate in certain tenses and in the reduplicated form of πίμπλημι pimplēmi to "fill" (literally or figuratively [imbue, influence, supply]); specifically to fulfil (time): - accomplish, full (. . . come), furnish.

NOTE: The word that jumps out at me from the definition of supply is the word "replete."

REPLETE (1) abundantly supplied or provided (2) filled (usually followed by with) (3) stuffed or gorged with food and drink. (4) Complete.

~Dictionary.com

"My God will abundantly supply and provide, fill with all that I need spiritually, emotionally, physically and complete me based on (according to) His riches in glory in Christ Jesus and their ain't no shortage in glory and in The Anointed One and His anointing."
~Philippians 4:19 with emphasis and additions mine
Ruminator Style, the Replete Version

2. What will your God supply for you? (Philippians 4:19)

3. What is God's supply based on? (Philippians 4:19)

4. Will He (God) meet your (1) Needs (2) Greed? (Philippians 4:19)

5. Why did Paul receive the money/gift that they sent Him? (Philippians 4:17)

6. How did He receive everything? (Philippians 4:18)

7. What did he have? (Philippians 4:18)

8. What did Paul consider the gift to be? (Philippians 4:18)

9. What was this acceptable sacrifice to God? (Philippians 4:18)

NOTE: This brings us back to the original verse in Philippians 4:19, *"My God shall supply all your needs according to His riches in glory in Christ Jesus."*

NOTE: For sure, He will meet your needs but I have found that He is gracious and sometimes meets our greed (selfish stuff) because of His mercy.

- THE SECRET (Philippians 4:11-13)

NOTE: Philippians 4:10-17 is the precursor to Philippians 4:19 where Paul had learned The Secret to *want*.

"...I have learned the secret..." (Philippians 4:10-17, Psalm 23:1)

NOTE: Paul was in prison in Rome as he wrote to the church in Philippi who had revived their concern for him and sent him a gift of money. He told them that He did not seek the gift itself, but;

> *"I sought the profit which increases to their account because they gave."*
> ~Philippians 4:17

1. What had the church revived? (Philippians 4:10)
2. What had they lacked, even though they were concerned? (Philippians 4:10)
3. What did Paul not speak from? (Philippians 4:11)
4. When the Lord is your Shepherd, what do you not do? (Psalm 23:1)

NOTE: I don't believe that the Lord does not restrict us from voicing our wants/needs. We do not speak from want/need because we know that we know that we *know* that He will supply ALL of our needs according to His riches in glory. As a matter of fact, the Lord knows what you want/need before you even ask, but He wants you to ask as you trust Him for everything in your life. (Matthew 6:8) I would say that if you don't have what you want/need, then you may need to check your relationship with your Shepherd, because as David the Psalmist/King states, "The Lord is my Shepherd, I...SHALL NOT...WANT!

5. What did Paul *not* speak from? (Philippians 4:11)

NOTE: See the previous note on want.

6. What had Paul learned? (Philippians 4:11)

CONTENT: autarkēs (ow-tar'-kace)= self-complacent, that is, contented: - content

SELF-COMPLACENT: (1)pleased, especially with oneself or one's merits (2) advantages, situation, etc., often without awareness of some potential danger or defect (3) self-satisfied (4) agreeable and eager to please.

7. When was Paul content? (Philippians 4:11)

CONTENT: (1) a condition, detail, part, or attribute, with respect to time, place, manner, agent, etc., that accompanies, determines, or modifies a fact or event (2) a modifying or influencing factor (3) the existing conditions or state of affairs surrounding and affecting an agent (4) an unessential or secondary accompaniment of any fact or event (5) the condition or state of a person with respect to income and material welfare:

    8. What had Paul learned? (Philippians 4:12)
    9. What could Paul do? (Philippians 4:13)
    10. What is this ability to do based on? (Philippians 4:13)
    NOTE: We tend to use Philippians 4:13 as our go to verse when we are faced with hard things, but this verse is in relationship to money and things. Later in Philippians 4:19 we see the source of supply. I like to title these two verses as my Strength (can do) and Supply (my God shall, my Pro-Vision)

    •   OPEN WINDOWS (Malachi 3:7-12)

> *"Bring the whole tithe into the storehouse, so that there may be food in My house and test me now in this, says the Lord of hosts; if I will not open for you the windows of heaven and pour out for you blessing until it overflows."*
>
>   ~Malachi 3:10

NOTE: "Two tithes were required: and annual tithe for the maintenance of the Levites (Leviticus 27:3, Numbers 18:21) and a second tithe brought to Jerusalem for the Lord's feast (Deuteronomy 14:22). Every third year, however, the second tithe was kept at home and used for the poor (Deuteronomy 14:28). One's use of money is often a barometer of his spirituality." (1 John 3:17)

    ~Commentary from Ryrie Study Bible on Malachi 3:10

NOTE: Back in the '70s we sang a song based on Malachi 3:10 called "The Windows Of Heaven." We sang about the windows of heaven being open and blessings falling and that there was joy in our hearts since *Jesus made everything right.* We then sang about giving Him our *old tattered garments* and in their place, *He gave us a robe of pure white.* As a result there was *joy in our hearts.*

1. What had Israel turned aside from and not done? (Malachi 3:7)

2. What was needed for them to do? (Malachi 3:7)

3. What question did they have? (Malachi 3:7)

4. What were they doing by turning aside from God's statues and not keeping them? (Malachi 3:8)

5. How were they robbing God? (Malachi 3:8)

a. _____

TITHES: ma'ăśêr ma'ăśar ma'aśrâh (mah-as-ayr', mah-as-ar', mah-as-raw')=From H6240; a tenth; especially a tithe: - tenth (part), tithe (-ing). H6240: 'âśâr (aw-sawr'=) For H6235; ten (only in combination), that is, the "teens"; also (ordinal) a "teenth": - [eigh-, fif-, four-, nine-, seven-, six-, thir-] teen (-th), + eleven (-th), + sixscore thousand, + twelve (-th).

b. _____

OFFERINGS: terûmâh terûmâh (ter-oo-maw', ter-oo-maw')=(The second form used in Deu_12:11); from H7311; a present (as offered up), especially in sacrifice or as tribute: - gift, heave offering ([shoulder]), oblation, offered (-ing). H7311: rûm (room)=A primitive root; to be high actively to rise or raise (in various applications, literally or figuratively): - bring up, exalt (self), extol, give, go up, haughty, heave (up), (be, lift up on, make on, set up on, too) high (-er, one), hold up, levy, lift (-er) up, (be) lofty, (X a-) loud, mount up, offer (up), + presumptuously, (be) promote (-ion), proud, set up, tall (-er), take (away, off, up), breed worms.

6. What was the cause and effect of robbing God of tithes and offerings? (Malachi 3:9)

7. Did individuals robbing God just affect themselves? If not, who? (Malachi 3:9)

8. How much of the tithe are we to bring to the storehouse? (Malachi 3:10)

9. Why should the tithe be brought into the storehouse?

10. What did God tell them to do about the tithe? (Malachi 3:10)

11. What would God do if they tested Him I the tithe? (Malachi 3:10)

12. What will be poured out from the widows of heaven? (Malachi 3:10)

NOTE: See Philippians 4:19 for what is found in His glory (His presence) and in Christ Jesus.

13. How long will the blessings be poured out? (Malachi 3:10)

NOTE: See Luke 6:38 about overflowing blessings.

14. What will God do when you quit robbing Him of the tithes and offerings? (Malachi 3:11)

15. Why will God rebuke the devourer for you? (Malachi 3:11)

16. What will all the nations call you? (Malachi 3:11)

17. Why will the nations call you blessed? (Malachi 3:11)

NOTE: Disobedience brings on the curse while obedience brings on the blessing. Jesus hanging on a tree, He became cursed in our place so that we might be blessed. (Galatians 3:10-14)

NOTE: Jesus said;

> *"Whoa to you, scribes, Pharisees, hypocrites! For you tithe mint and dill and cumin, and have neglected the weightier provisions of the law; justice and mercy and faithfulness; but these are the thing you should have done without neglecting the other."*
> ~Matthew 23:23, Luke 11:42

NOTE: Tithing is most definitely an Old Testament Principle. In the New Testament tithing is not negated. Those who were Jews under the old covenant were encouraged to tithe. Jesus had a problem with them doing legalistic tithing while missing the point of meeting the needs of people.

I personally believe that tithing is a good thing to do, but giving generously is what we need to be doing. I believe that we have been released from the tithe to be givers. I believe for us (me and Brenda) tithing is a good starting place, but we springboard into giving to others. I know people who don't tithe but the amount of money that they give to the church and to others in need far exceeds their tithe. Many people try to see how little they can get away with in their giving.

NOTE: It appears to me that we *pay a tithe* and *give an offering*. Either way, it all comes from Him as we will see in 2 Corinthians 9:6-12 that God gives the seed for us to sow.

- CAUSE AND EFFECT OF SOWING SEED (2 Corinthians 9:6-12)

"Now this I say, he who sows sparingly will also reap sparingly, and he who sows bountifully will also reap bountifully."
~2 Corinthians 9:6

NOTE: With the next three sections we will talk about the cause and effect of giving and receiving, sowing and reaping and the cause and effect on our prosperity and success.

1. What is the cause and effect of someone sowing sparingly? (2 Corinthians 9:6)

2. What is the cause and effect of someone sowing bountifully? (2 Corinthians 9:6)

NOTE: This particular passage is using the analogy of farming, planting seeds, and reaping harvest. The connection of the context is sowing money into the lives of the poor saints in Jerusalem. (See Romans 15:26-27)

3. In the principles of sowing money, what must each one do? (2 Corinthians 9:7)

4. What must each one *not* do? (2 Corinthians 9:7)

5. What does God love? (2 Corinthians 9:7)

CHEERFUL: hilaros (hil-ar-os')=From the same as G2436; propitious or merry ("hilarious"), that is, prompt or willing: - cheerful. G2436: hileōs (hil'-eh-oce)=; cheerful (as attractive), that is, propitious; adverbially (by Hebraism) God be gracious!, that is, (in averting some calamity) far be it: - be it far, merciful.

NOTE: God loves the world, no matter how they act. He loved

the world enough to send His only begotten, unique Son to die for the world before they ever believed or accepted Him. When it says God loves a "cheerful giver" it is in the context of the manner of giving. I believe that it shows how much the believer trusts in God, even with their money, because they know that they will receive back more than they gave out.

6. What is God able to do? (2 Corinthians 9:8)

7a. When we have all grace abounding to us, what will we always have? (2 Corinthians 9:8)

ALL SUFFICIENCY: autarkeia (ow-tar'-ki-ah)=From G842; self satisfaction, that is, (abstractly) contentedness, or (concretely) a competence: - contentment, sufficiency. G842: autarkēs (ow-tar'-kace)= self complacent, that is, contented: - content.

7b. When we have all sufficiency in everything, what may we have? (2 Corinthians 9:8)

ABUNDANCE: perisseuō (per-is-syoo'-o)=From G4053; to super-abound (in quantity or quality), be in excess, be superfluous; also (transitively) to cause to superabound or excel: - (make, more) abound, (have, have more) abundance, (be more) abundant, be the better, enough and to spare, exceed, excel, increase, be left, redound, remain (over and above). G4053: perissos (per-is-sos')=From G4012 (in the sense of beyond); superabundant (in quantity) or superior (in quality); by implication excessive; adverb (with G1537) violently; neuter (as noun) preeminence: - exceeding abundantly above, more abundantly, advantage, exceedingly, very highly, beyond measure, more, superfluous, vehement [-ly]. G4012: peri (per-ee')=From the base of G4008; properly through (all over), that is, around; figuratively with respect to; used in various applications, of place, cause or time (with the genitive case denoting the subject or occasion or superlative point; with the accusative case the locality, circuit, matter, circumstance or general period): - (there-) about, above, against, at, on behalf of, X and his company, which concern, (as) concerning, for, X how it will go with, ([there-, where-]) of, on, over, pertaining (to), for sake, X (e-) state, (as) touching, [where-] by (in), with. In compounds it retains substantially the same meaning of circuit (around), excess (beyond), or completeness (through).G4004: peran (per'-an)=Apparently the accusative case of an obsolete derivation of πείρω peirō (to "pierce"); through (as adverb or preposition), that is, across: - beyond, farther (other) side, over.

NOTE: This thing called ABUNDANCE has meanings like (1) to super abound (2) be in excess (3) be superfluous (4) superabundant (5) superior in quality (6) excessive, just to name a view concepts of abundance. This is far from what is known as "trickledown economics" of the world.

8. What purpose is this abundance? (2 Corinthians 9:8)

9. What does God supply for the sower? (2 Corinthian 9:10)

10. What does God supply bread for? (2 Corinthians 9:10)

11. What will God supply and multiply your seed for? (2 Corinthians 9:10)

12. As He supplies your seed for sowing what will He increase? (2 Corinthians 9:10)

13. As you sow and reap in the natural, what type of harvest will you increase? (2 Corinthians 9:10)

14. What will you be enriched in? (2 Corinthians 9:11)

15. What will you be enriched in everything for? (2 Corinthians 9:11)

BOUNDIFUL/LIBERALITY: haplotēs (hap-lot'-ace)=From G573; singleness, that is, (subjectively) sincerity (without dissimulation or self seeking), or (objectively) generosity (copious bestowal): - bountifulness, liberal (-ity), simplicity, singleness. G573: haplous (hap-looce')=; properly folded together, that is, single (figuratively clear): - single.

16. What does our giving/sowing produce through us? (2 Corinthians 9:11)

NOTE: Our natural act of giving produces a spiritual act, thanksgiving (the giving of thanks) to God.

17. What is giving considered to be? (2 Corinthians 9:12)

18. What is the ministry of this service (of giving) fully supplying? (2 Corinthians 9:12)

19. What is the ministry of this service (of giving) not only fully supplying the needs of the saints, but overflowing with what? (2 Corinthians 9:12)

> *"Because of the proof given by this ministry, they will glorify God for your obedience to your confession of the gospel of Christ and for the LIBERALITY of your CONTRIBUTION to them and to all, while they also, by PRAYER on your behalf, yearn for you because of the surpassing grace of God in you."*
>
> ~2 Corinthians 9:13-14 emphasis mine

20. What is this liberal contribution described as? (2 Corinthians 9:15)

NOTE: This liberal contribution goes beyond a normal tithe, it breaks into the realm of giving.

• THE STANDARED OF MEASURE OF GIVING

> *"Give and it will be given to you. They will pour into your lap a good measure, pressed down, shaken together, and running over. For by your standard of measure it will be measured to you in return."*
>
> ~Luke 6:38

NOTE: Jesus is teaching what has become known as the Sermon on the Mount (found in Matthew 5-7). Some believe it could also be a similar teaching known as The Golden Rule:

> *"Treat others the same way you want them to treat you."*
>
> ~Luke 6:31

The idea of giving out what you want to receive back is introduced. Some call this the law of sowing and reaping, the law of reciprocity, the law of seedtime and harvest, or seed faith. We will cover this more in depth in Galatians 6:7-10)

NOTE: Jesus speaks about how we are not to give just to get. Even sinners do that. (Luke 6:30-36) Even though Jesus teaches that we don't give to get, the principle and law of reciprocity is still working as when we give, we get back in return, in like kind.

1. What happens when you love your enemies and do good, and lend, expecting nothing in return? (Luke 6:34)

2. How is God our example in these things? (Luke 6:35)

3. How shall we be merciful? (Luke 6:35)

4. What happens if we *do not* judge? (Luke 6:27)

5. What will happen if we *do not* condemn? (Luke 6:37)

NOTE: Have you ever heard someone say, "Don't judge me" or the Bible (or Jesus) says to *not* condemn others. When people believe they are being judged or condemned, they are quick to bring Matthew 7:1 up in our face. Of course, this is a misquotation of the Bible.

"Do not judge so that your will not be judged, for in the way you judge you will be judged; and by your standard of measure, it will be measured to you". Why do you look at the speck that is in your brother's eye, but do not notice the log that is in your own eye? Or how can you say to your brother, Let me take the speck out of your eye, and behold, the log is in your own eye?
~Matthew 7:1-4

That seems correct *if* you leave out Matthew 7:5.

"You hypocrite, FIRST take the log out of your own eye, and THEN you will see clearly to take the speck out of your brother's eye."
~Matthew 7:5 emphasis mine

NOTE: This is not a passage about not condemning or judging someone, but a passage on how to condemn or judge *properly*. We must first have a LOGECTOMY in our own eyes before we attempt to have a SPECTECTOMY in someone else's eye, because the law of reciprocity will be working, and we will get back what we do.

6. Paul writes to the Church of God in Corinth for those who are sinning with sexual immorality and negative people and actually

dealing with outsiders and those within the church. (See 1 Corinthians 5:3-11)

> *"For what have I (Paul, a Christian) to do with JUDGING outsiders? Do you not JUDGE those who are within the church? But those who are outside God JUDGES, remove the wicked man from among ourselves."*
> ~1 Corinthians 5:12-13 emphasis and addition mine

NOTE: Paul goes on to speak of Christians judging others in the afterlife. (1 Corinthians 6:1-8) So, the law of reciprocity kicks in when we don't first deal with our sins before speaking in someone else's life.

7. What will happen *if* we pardon? (Luke 6:37)

NOTE: Now we see the standard of measurement given back to you based on how you give.

> *"Give, and it shall be given unto you; good measure, pressed down, and shaken together, and running over, shall men give into your bosom. For with the same measure that ye mete withal it shall be measured to you again."*
> ~Luke 6:38 KJV

> *"Give, and it will be given to you. They will pour into your lap a good measure—pressed down, shaken together, and running over. For by your standard of measure it will be measured to you in return."*
> ~Luke 6:38

> *"Give, and [gifts] will be given to you; good measure, pressed down, shaken together, and running over will they pour into [the pouch formed by] the bosom [of your robe and used as a bag]. For with THE MEASURE YOU DEAL OUT, [with the measure you use when you confer benefits on others], it WILL BE MEASURED BACK TO YOU."*
> ~Luke 6:38 AMP emphasis mine

NOTE: We will look closer at the cause and effect of sowing and reaping with Galatians 6:7-10.

8. What will happen when you give (good)? (Luke 6:38)

9. What measure will they (other humans) pour into your lap? (Luke 6:38)

10. After they (other humans) have given you a good (fair) measure, what will they do? (Luke 6:38)

11. What do they (other humans) do with the good measure that is pressed down to make room for more? (Luke 6:38)

12. What is the end result as they keep on giving to you? (Luke 6:38)

13. Who will pour into your lap (clothing gathered together to make a basket)? (Luke 6:38)

14. What will your return be based upon? (Luke 6:38)

RECIPROCITY: SOWING, REAPING, HARVEST (Galatians 6:7-10)

"Do not be deceived, God is not mocked; for whatever a man sows this shall he also reap."

~Galatians 6:7

NOTE: We continue to look at the law of reciprocity in connection with what you sow (good, bad, or ugly).

1. What should we *not be* concerning sowing and reaping? (Galatians 6:7)

DECEIVED: planaō (plan-ah'-o)=From G4106; to (properly cause to) roam (from safety, truth, or virtue): - go astray, deceive, err, seduce, wander, be out of the way G4106: planē (plan'-ay)=Feminine of G4108 (as abstraction); objectively fraudulence; subjectively a straying from orthodoxy or piety: - deceit, to deceive, delusion, error. G4108: planos (plan'-os)=Of uncertain affinity; roving (as a tramp), that is, (by implication) an impostor or misleader: - deceiver, seducing.

NOTE: Apparently a person can be led astray about issues of reciprocity.

2. In our deception, what is God *not*? (Galatians 6:7)

MOCKED: muktērizō (mook'-tay-rid'-zo)=From a derivative of the base of G3455 (meaning snout, as that whence lowing proceeds from); to make mouths at, that is, ridicule: - mock. G3455: mukaomai (moo-kah'-om-ahe)=From a presumed derivative of μύζω muzō (to "moo"); to bellow (roar): - roar.

NOTE: Have you ever heard how people respond to the truth of reciprocity, sowing and reaping, giving and receiving, seedtime and harvest? They not only mock God, but they mock the people who believe God concerning these matters.

3. What is the cause of whatever a man sows? (Galatians 6:7)

WHATSOEVER/WHATEVER; ean (eh-an')= a conditional particle; in case that, provided, etc.; often used in connection with other particles to denote indefiniteness or uncertainty: - before, but, except, (and) if, (if) so, (what-, whither-) soever, though, when (-soever), whether (or), to whom, [who-] so (-ever).

NOTE: Whatever includes good, bad, or ugly. The soil in which a seed is sown is no respecter of seeds. *If* you sow seeds of corn, the soil receives it and produces like kind. *If* you sow seeds of poison ivy, the soil receives it and produces like kind. *If* you sow flowers, the soil receives it and produces beautiful flowers. *If* you sow seeds of kudzu, the soil will receive it and produce vegetation that will overtake everything around it.

NOTE TO THE NOTE: I personally like the ways kudzu looks. Yes, it is incessant in taking over everything from ditches, to trees, to power line posts etc.

> *"For they have sown the wind, and they shall reap the whirlwind: it hath no stalk: the bud shall yield no meal: if so be it yield, the strangers shall swallow it up."*
>
> ~Hosea 8:7

"For they sow the wind and they shall reap the whirlwind. The standing grain has no heads; and it shall yield no meal; if it were to yield, strangers and aliens would eat it up."

~Hosea 8:7 AMP

4. What happens when you sow to the wind? (Hosea 7:8)

5. What happens to the seed production? (Hosea 7:8)

a. _____

b. _____

6. What if the seed does yield fruit? (Hosea 7:8)

7. What will the one who sows to the flesh do? (Galatians 6:8)

8. What will the one who sows to the Spirit do? (Galatians 6:8)

NOTE: The harvest is based on two factors: (1) The Seed (2) The Soil.

NOTE TO THE NOTE: For full insights for sowing and reaping see the *Parable Of The Sower, Seed, And Soil.* (Mark 4:1-20, Matthew 13:1-15, Luke 8:4-10)

9. What are we *not* to lose? (Galatians 6:9)

10. Why should we *not lose heart* in doing good (not bad)? (Galatians 6:9)

11. What is need from us for us to reap? (Galatians 6:9)

12. What do we need to do while we have opportunity? (Galatians 6:10)

NOTE: This sowing is not only to *all* people.

13. Who should we especially sow good seed in good soil to so we can reap a good harvest? (Galatians 6:10)

• KINGDOM DESIRES MET (Matthew 6: 25-35)

"But seek (continuously) first His kingdom and His righteousness, and all these (tangible) tings will be added to you."

~Matthew 6:33 addition mine

Giving and receiving, sowing and reaping are Kingdom Principles where the King has implemented laws in the universe that we use in this world but are rooted in heaven. These can be like the law of gravity that works for both Christians and non-Christians alike. I believe that utilizing these principles will affect our prosperity and success.

- KINGDOM DEFINED:

  "The Kingdom of God is not meat nor drink (the tangibles of this world) but righteousness (equity of character or act; specifically (Christian) justification) peace (prosperity: - one, peace, quietness, rest, + set at one again) and joy (cheerfulness, calm delight, gladness) in the Holy Ghost."

  ~Romans 14:17 addition mine

KINGDOM: basileia (bas-il-i'-ah)=From G935; properly royalty, that is, (abstractly) rule, or (concretely) a realm (literally or figuratively): - kingdom, + reign.G935: basileus (bas-il-yooce')=Probably from G939 (through the notion of a foundation of power); a sovereign (abstractly, relatively or figuratively): - king. G939: basis (bas'-ece)=From βαίνω bainō (to walk); a pace ("base"), that is, (by implication) the foot: - foot.

NOTE: To have a kingdom there must be a King, the one in control. The Kingdom of God has the King and His Son. This Kingdom is not one of a forced overthrow, but one of free-will submission. This Kingdom has laws/principle that when followed it will yield prosperity and success. This Kingdom is defined by:
  a. Royalty
  b. Rule
  c. A Realm
  d. Reign
  e. A Foundation of Power
  f. Sovereign
  g. To Walk
  h. A Pace
  i. The Foot.
NOTE: In karate, the key to throwing a good technique, a kick,

punch, block is a good foundation, a good stance with the feet planted. So it is with principles/laws of the Kingdom of God. A firm foundation plus repetition, repetition, repetition of the correct technique brings prosperity and success.

1. What should we not be, about our life? (Matthew 6:25)

2. What does our lives consist of? (Matthew 6:25)

a. _____

b. _____

c. _____

d. _____

3. What is life more than and the body more than? (Matthew 6:25)

a. _____

b. _____

4. What do the birds NOT do? (Matthew 6:26)

a. _____

b. _____

c. _____

5. What does the heavenly Father do for the birds? (Matthew 6:26)

6. Who is worth more than the birds? (Matthew 6:26)

7. What can worrying *not* do? (Matthew 6:27)

8. What do you need to do if you are worrying about clothing? (Matthew 6:28)

9. What does the lilies of the field do not do? (Matthew 6:28)

a. _____

b. _____

10. How did Solomon's clothing compare to the lilies of the field? (Matthew 6:29)

11. If God clothes the grass of the fields (which is alive today and tomorrow is thrown into the furnace, what will God much more do for you? (Matthew 6:30)

12. When we worry about life, what we will eat and drink, what we will put on our body, what is that worry a sign of? (Matthew 6:30)

13. How much faith (what size of faith) is required to speak to a mountain (an immovable object) and tell it to move and where to go? (Matthew 11:22-23, Luke 12:6)

14. How much faith was given to those who believe? (Romans 12:3)

15. What did Jesus tell us *not* to do? (Matthew 6:31)

16. What should we not be? (Philippians 4:6)

NOTE: The things that we should not be anxious for are *nothing* and *everything*. (Philippians 4:6)

17 Name three things should we do *instead* of worrying/being anxious? (Philippians 4:6)

    a. _____

    b. _____

    c. _____

PRAYER: proseuchē (pros-yoo-khay')=From G4336; prayer (worship); by implication an oratory (chapel): - X pray earnestly, prayer. G4336: proseuchomai (pros-yoo'-khom-ahee)= to pray to God, that is, supplicate, worship: - pray (X earnestly, for), make prayer.

NOTE: The bottom line is that prayer is conversing with God, having a conversation, talking and listening to one another

SUPPLICATION: deēsis (deh'-ay-sis)=From G1189; a petition: - prayer, request, supplication. G1189: deomaideh'-om-ahee =to beg (as binding oneself), that is, petition: - beseech, pray (to), make request.

THANKSGIVING: eucharistia (yoo-khar-is-tee'-ah)=From G2170; gratitude; actually grateful language (to God, as an act of worship): - thankfulness, (giving of) thanks (-giving). G2170: eucharistos (yoo-khar'-is-tos)=well favored, that is, (by implication) grateful: - thankful.

NOTE: Anxiety/Worrying can be busted by faith as we pray (talk to God), supplicate (be humbly specific with your request) and give thanks before we see the answer. This will cause the peace (no worries) of God that surpasses all comprehension to guard your heart and your mind in Christ (the Anointed One and His anointing). (Philippians 4:7)

18. What must we do for this to take place? (Philippians 4:6)

NOTE: If we don't LET/ALLOW our request to be made known

to God (even though He already knows what we need before we ask), then we will continue to be anxious/worried.

16. What should we not say? (Matthew 6:31)

a. _____

b. _____

c. _____

18. Who eagerly seeks the things listed in Matthew 6:31?

NOTE: The Gentiles were Non-Covenant/Promise people. The Jews were Covenant/Promise people who had everything they needed. When you become a follower of Jesus by believing in the work He did on the Cross/Tree, we become Covenant People and don't have to worry about anything. (Galatians 3:10-14) True Biblical Prosperity and Success is hinged on our relationship with The Word. (Joshua 1:8, John 1:1-4)

19. What does the heavenly Father already know? (Matthew 6:32, Matthew 6:8)

NOTE: He knows what we need, He wants to give them to us, but He wants us to please Him by coming to Him and acknowledging that He is a rewarder (a giver) to those who diligently seek Him (Hebrews 11:6)

20. What should we keep on seeking first? (Matthew 6:33)

a. _____

b. _____

21. What will be added when you seek His kingdom and righteousness first? (Matthew 6:33)

22. What do we *not* have to do? (Matthew 6:34)

23. What will take care of itself? (Matthew 6:34)

24. What does each day have enough of? (Matthew 6:34)

NOTE: Why waste time worrying about God's Pro-Vision?

• THE ART OF ASKING (James 4:2-3)

"...You do not HAVE because you do not ASK."

~James 4:2

NOTE: Some Christians, denominations, and theologians teach

that we are not supposed to ask God for anything. *If* God wants us to have it, He will give it. Then, *If* we do ask and do not get it, then it is God's will (wish, desire) for us NOT to have it and then we call that the "sovereignty of God" on earth as it is in heaven. So instead of asking we just accept the d-evil's will on earth as it is in hell.

1. What is the source of quarrels and conflicts among you? (James 4:1)

LUSTS: hēdonē (hay-don-ay')=From ἀνδάνω handanō (to please); sensual delight; by implication desire: - lust, pleasure.

2. What is in the world (that many love)? (1 John 2:16)

a. _____

b. _____

c. _____

NOTE: These are the things that the d-evil uses in temptation with Adam and Eve, with Jesus, with you and me, and every other person in the world. Temptation is not primarily used to pull you into or entice you into something *but* to pull you away from who you are in Christ and away from your destiny, purpose, and future. I believe that the d-evil and the lust in us pulls us away from true Biblical Prosperity and Success.

2. When you (or anyone) is tempted, are they being tempted (enticed to evil) by God? James 1:13)

3. Can God be tempted by evil? (James 1:13)

4. Does God tempted (entice to evil) anyone? (James 1:13)

5. How are we tempted (James 1:14)

6. What is the progression to death? (James 1:15)

a. Lust conceived

b. Gives birth to sin

c. Sin is accomplished

d. Brings forth death

NOTE: This is the first time that L.S.D. is mentioned in the Bible

L=lust

S=sin

D=death

2. What does the war waged in you members look like? (James 4:1-2)

a. _____

b. _____

3. Why do you not have? (James 4:2)

4. Why do you not receive when you ask? (James 4:3)

5. When you don't receive, what do you do with the wrong motives? (James 4:3)

NOTE: This asking with wrong motives goes back to sowing and reaping, sow wrong motives, reap nothing but troubles, quarrels, and conflicts among you and other people.

- THE TENACITY OF ASKING (Matthew 17:7-11, Luke 11:9-13

"Ask, and it will be given to you, seek, and you will find; knock and it will be opened to you."

~Matthew 17:7, Luke 11:9

NOTE: The meaning in the Greek for ask, seek knock is *Keep On Asking, Keeping On Seeking, And Keep On Knocking.*

NOTE: The traditional method of prayer is to ask once and if you don't get you answer, then quit asking because God said No! So, we give up asking, give up seeking, and give up on knocking.

1. What is the cause and effect of keeping on asking? (Matthew 17:7)

2. What is the cause and effect of keeping on seeking? (Matthew 17:7)

3. What is the cause and effect of keeping on knocking? (Matthew 17:7)

4. What happens to everyone who keeps on asking? (Matthew 17:8)

5. What happens to everyone who keeps on seeking? (Matthew 17:8)

6. What happens to everyone who keeps on knocking? (Matthew 17:8)

NOTE: Jesus uses and example from real life in regards to asking, seeking and knocking?

7. What will a man/father *not* give a son if he asks for a loaf of bread? (Matthew 17:9)

8. What will a man/father *not* give a son if he asks for a fish? Matthew 17:10)

9. IF you, an evil man, knows how to give good gifts to your son, how does that compare to your Father who is in heaven? (Matthew 17:11)

NOTE: Luke 11:13 speaks about the Father giving you the Holy Spirit (not some counterfeit demons/d-evil to those who keep on asking, seeking and knocking. It does not matter if you are asking for spiritual things, emotional things, physical things, financial things, if you see it in the Word of God, KEEP ON ASKING, and SEEK-ING, and KNOCKING.

- PESISTENCE IN ASKING (Luke 11:1-13 Luke 18:1-8)

"Then He (Jesus teaching on prayer) to them (His disciples) sup-pose one of you has a friend and goes to him at midnight and says to him at midnight and say to him, friend, lend me three loaves."
~Luke 11:5

"Now He (Jesus) was telling them a parable to show that AT ALL TIMES they ought to PRAY and NOT TO LOSE HEART (give up)."
~Luke 18:1 emphasis and addition mine

NOTE: Back in the days of the charismatic/Spirit filled move-ment, it was taught that if we pray for something ten times, then nine of those times of prayer was out of unbelief. If we *really* believed that God was going to answer our prayers, then we need to pray once and then thank God until the manifestation/answer comes. That sounds pretty good, but that is not what Jesus taught us concerning prayer.

1. How should we pray at all times? (Luke 18:1)

2. When we pray and don't see an answer, what should we *not* do? (Luke 18:1)

3. Who was in a certain city? (Luke 18:1)

4. What was the judge's attitude towards God? (Luke 18:2)

5. Who did the judge not respect? (Luke 18:2)

6. Where do we have favor and good repute/report with? (Pro-Verbs 3:4)

NOTE: Even when we are faced with someone (like the judge) who does not fear God and does not respect man, we can and do have favor and respect with people like the judge, *if* we don't give up.

7. What did the widow in the city do? (Luke 18:3)

8. What was the widow's request? (Luke 18:3)

9. Was the judge willing or unwilling at her first request? (Luke 18:4)

10. What did the judge decide to do even if he did not fear God or respect man/humans? (Luke 18:5)

11. What was the widow considered to be by the judge? (Luke 18:5)

12. Why did the judge decide to give the widow legal protection? (Luke 18:8)

NOTE: The widow continually came to the judge, who had what she needed. By continually coming to the judge, she wore him out. Remember, this is a parable on prayer and how we should approach God (who holds our answers). God gives us permission to wear Him out. He can handle it.

13. What will God *not* hold out on us, *if* we cry to Him day and night? (Luke 18:6-7)

14. What *will* God do for us *if* we cry to Him day and night? (Luke 18:8)

15. What is the Son of Man expecting to find when He comes? (Luke 18:8)

NOTE: Prayer is a *faith issue*, if we want to please God.

> *"Without FAITH (towards God, Hebrews 11:6) it is impossible to please Him, for, he who comes to God must believe that He is and that He is a rewarder of those who (diligently) (keeping on) seeking Him and not just passively inquire of Him."*
> ~Hebrew 11:6 emphasis and additions mine
> Ruminator Style

• OCEAN WAVES DELIVERY SYSTEM (Ecclesiastes 11:1-10)

NOTE: This passage is about successful prospects of a bold business venture as there is wisdom in diversified investment. (From the Ryrie Bible study notes on Ecclesiastes 11:1-2)

NOTE: Solomon, the wisest and richest man at the time knew the gains and pitfalls of riches, prosperity and success. The Book of Pro-Verbs is a book of Positive Actions to take as we live our lives.

"Cast thy bread upon the waters: for thou shalt find it after many days."

~Ecclesiastes 11:1 KJV

"Send your grain across the seas, and in time, profits will flow back to you."

~Ecclesiastes 11:1 NLT

"Cast (sow) your bread (seed) upon the water (soil) for thou (the bread/seed caster) shalt find it (bread/seed) after many days (time frame)."

~Ecclesiastes 11:1 emphasis and additions mine
Ruminator Style

"Cast your bread on the surface of the waters, [be diligently active, make thoughtful decisions], for you will find it after many days."

Ecclesiastes 11:1 AMP

1. Whose bread are you casting? (Ecclesiastes 11:1)
2. Who is responsible for the casting? (Ecclesiastes 11:1)
3. Where are you casting the bread? (Ecclesiastes 11:1)
4. What will you find after many days?

NOTE: I love to go to the beach/ocean and sit under an umbrella with my toes in the sand and watch and listen to the ebb and flow of the waters. I love the rhythmic in and out of the waves, seaweed, various objects, and yes, people. They swim out, and as the waves flow in, the people flow out. I like to imagine praying to God specific needs, and as the waves go out, I receive back the answers with the incoming waves.

"To cast one's bread upon the waters is an expression that means to give generously without worrying about what you will gain from

it or what the people will do with what you give them."
~writingexplained.org

"Divide your portion to seven, or even to eight, for you do not know what misfortune may occur on the earth."
~Ecclesiastes 11:2

NOTE: Ecclesiastes 11:1-2 speaks from a prosperous and successful perspective of diversified investments and how investors (bread casters) can expect a return on their investment. The is wisdom in not investing all of your bread on one wave, but to diversify, because you never know what the next day will bring. We don't know what calamity will take place from day to day, however we are not called to fear but be wise. I believe the various portions that we divide are like having M.S.I.s (Multiple Sources of Income).

NOTE TO THE NOTE: There are many types of bread that can be cast (invested), including sourdough, whole wheat, pumpernickel, rye, etc. This correlates to types of seeds that can be sown, with an expectation that whatever type of seed that you have sown (cast onto the waters) can be expected to produce a harvest. There is no need to be surprised about the harvest. Sow corn, get corn. Sow poison ivy, get poison ivy.

"Don't be surprised when you sow poison ivy that you get a rash."
~Rodfucious, ancient sage with quirky wit and wisdom

"That which has been is that which will be, and that which has been done is that which will be done, so there is nothing new under the sun."
~Ecclesiastes 1:9

- FISH BANKS ON THE BANKS OF THE SEA

"So that we do not offend them (tax collectors/), to the sea and throw in a hook, and take the first fish that comes up; and when you open its (the fish) mouth, you will find a shekel, take that and

give it to them (tax collectors) for you (Rodney Lewis Boyd) and me (Jesus)."

~Matthew 17:27

1. What was the need that was demanded from the tax-gatherer? (Matthew 7:24)

2. Who else other than Peter owed the tax? (Matthew 7:24)

3. What did Jesus say about who should pay taxes? (Matthew 7:25)

NOTE: The answer was that kings of the earth collects customs, poll-tax, from their sons—not strangers. Sons were exempt from taxes.

4. What did Jesus not want to do to the king and collectors of the taxes? (Matthew 7:27)

5. What three things did Jesus tell Peter? (Matthew 7:27)

a. _____

b. _____

c. _____

6. What will Peter find? (Matthew 7:27)

NOTE: Jesus and Peter were exempt from taxes, but in order to not offend, Jesus chose to pay what they did not owe. It reminds me of Jesus hanging on the cross for offenses that He did not commit, but He paid the price anyway for you and me. That is called Amazing Grace.

NOTE TO THE NOTE: The American way is to protest taxes. God's way, don't offend, pay them what they ask, but realize that God is our Pro-Vider of Pro-Vision. The fish had a shekel in its mouth which was equal to two half-shackles, which covered taxes for Jesus and Peter (I don't know about the others). When in Israel we went to lunch at a restaurant that served Saint Peter's fish (the whole fish, friend, with the head still on it).

NOTE TO THE NOTE TO THE NOTE: We need to realize that most likely that shekel did not just miraculously appear in the fish's mouth, but before the situation arose, the fish had been prepared along the way to swallow the shekel. How much more does God know what you need before you even ask? (Matthew 6:8)

CHAPTER SIXTEEN

FINAL THOUGHTS...FINALLY
I BELIEVE (trust in, cling to, rely on, adhere to, cleave to) GOD'S HEARTBEAT FOR PROSPERITY AND GOOD SUCCESS

If you have not got it yet, I believe the will of God is for you and me to be prosperous and successful versus being in poverty and a failure. I don't believe that it is a mystery or secret that God is trying to keep from us. I do believe that the d-evil, the author of lies and confusion, is trying to keep us from living the abundant life that Jesus gave us. I believe that the d-evil came for the purpose to steal, kill, and destroy our physical lives and our spiritual lives. (John 10:10) I believe that the d-evil came to steal our desires, kill our visions and destroy our dreams. (John 10:10) I believe that Jesus (God in the flesh, John 1:1-14) came from heaven to give us life (and not death) and that life is to be abundant and not a life of mediocrity. (John 10:10)

Rodney, what do you really believe about Prosperity And Success Ruminator Style?

I really do believe that God gave us the power, dynamic, miraculous ability to make wealth and with that wealth there would be no sorrows. (Deuteronomy 8:18, Pro-Verbs 10:22)

I believe that money/riches/wealth is not evil, but the lust after money/riches/wealth is the root of all kinds of evil and that men fall away from the Lord when they become entangled with the root. (I Timothy 6:10)

I truly believe that John's true desire for believers is that we would prosper (have enough to meet our needs and an overflow to help others), be in health (physical and spiritual health), and to prosper (accomplish all of God's purposes in our lives). (3 John 2)

I know in my hearts of hearts that we have been released from the tithe into being a giver. Yes, I believe in the spiritual law of reciprocity that manifest itself in the physical realm as I give knowing it will be given back to me and not only given back the same amount but a return of good measure, pressed down, shaken together, running over, shall men (human beings used as instruments of God) give into my bosom/lap/life. (Luke 6:38)

As I stand at the edge of the waters of my life, I will cast my bread on the waters with great expectancy that on every wave that comes back to the shore, there will bread in return. (Ecclesiastes 11:1) I believe that there many types of bread, and depending on the type of bread that I cast I will receive that type of bread back.

I believe in the principle of sowing and reaping that works for money, negative or positive attitude, evil or good, poison or fresh waters. I really do believe that whatsoever (whatever it is) a man (man, wo-man, hu-man) sows (by thoughts, words, and actions) that person will reap back what is sown. I believe that sowing and reaping (corn or poison ivy) will be received by the soil/heart/universe, and the soil is no respecter of seed and will produce what is sown. (Galatians 6:7-8)

I believe God's Word when it tells us that when we sow sparingly we will reap sparingly (in reference and context to money we give for others), and that when we sow bountifully we will reap bountifully. (2 Corinthians 9:6)

I don't believe that God manipulates us to give so we end up giving grudgingly, but I believe that God loves a hilarious, cheerful giver. (2 Corinthians 9:7)

I believe that God gave us the free will, volition ability to choose what to give. We must purpose in our own hearts (give on purpose) what to give. (2 Corinthians 9:7)

I believe that we have the power of choice of what to give like Ananias had when he sold his land and held back part of the money secretly as he gave money. (Acts 5:1-11)

I believe that God has all sufficiency and is able to make all grace abound to me so I can have all sufficiency in everything and abundance for every good deed. (2 Corinthians 9:8)

I believe that God supplies seed for the sower (even the seed that

I sow is from God that He will multiply back to me to meet my needs and more seed to sow) as I get into the rhythm of giving. (2 Corinthians 9:10)

Yes, I believe that God will take the seed that I sow and supply and multiply my seed for sowing and increase the harvest of my righteousness, as the spiritual touches my physical life. I thank God that in everything for all liberality that God is producing thanksgiving to God through me. Praise God that I do not have to speak from a position of wanting/lusting because the Lord is my Shepherd. I shall not want because He has a never ending supply for me. My paradigm of prosperity and success thinks, speaks, and acts from a position of supply from God. (Philippians 4:10-11, Psalm 23:1)

I have learned from past experience with God how to be content (not anxious, fearful, full of dread or doubt) but I know that whatever circumstance I find myself in, whether I have little or have a lot, whether I am in prosperity (have an overflow) or going hungry, of having an abundance or suffering need, that I can do all things (with physical needs or spiritual needs) through Christ the Anointed One who infuses inner strength into me making me self-sufficient in Christ's sufficiency. (Philippians 4:12-13)

I know that I know that I know that my God will liberally supply, fill to the full, my every need according to, based on His riches in glory in Christ Jesus and their AIN'T no shortage in glory or Christ Jesus. (Philippians 4:19)

I believe that we are called to be blessed and not cursed. I believe that by the cross of Jesus we were translated/transported from the domain of darkness (where the d-evil dominated us into the Kingdom of Light (where we were set free) form "slaveation to salvation." (Colossians 1:13-14)

I believe that I (and so do you) have a choice of choosing blessing and life versus choosing a curse and death. (Deuteronomy 30:31, Deuteronomy chapters 28-30)

That is just a thumbnail sketch of what I believe concerning *Biblical Prosperity and Success Ruminator Style*.

This is the end of the book, but it is only the beginning of living life more abundantly.

RECOMMENDED RUMINATOR READING

In research for *Biblical Prosperity and Success Ruminator Style* I have read and researched many books, listened to many audios, and talked with many people to formulate these concepts. I want to recommend to you some of my resources so you can build a resource library also. Normally, when people create a listing of books they will give you the publisher's name, or point you in the direction where you can purchase the books. I am not going to do that, because I want you to take ownership and seek out these products on your own. You will only value what you are willing to invest financially and with your time.

1. *The Bible*: I believe *The Bible* is the #1 book on prosperity and success. *The Bible* is a library consisting of 66 books written by 40+ men under the inspiration of the Holy Spirit. If you don't have a firm foundation in the Bible (which will take years) you will only have a limited understanding of Biblical Success and Prosperity Ruminator Style.

2. *How To Live A Maximized Lifestyle by Rodney Boyd: Biblical Success and Prosperity Ruminator Style* is the sequel to my previous book. Thematically they are similar but both are great individual reads.

3. *Think and Grow Rich* by Napoleon Hill: I believe this is a classic book that not only covers being rich financially but being rich spiritually. Andrew Carnegie, once the richest man in the world, commissioned Napoleon to research and interview successful men like Thomas Edison, Henry Ford and many others about the secrets to their success. The results was a book called *Law of Success* from which Mr. Hill gleaned the thirteen principles in *Think and Grow Rich*.

4. *The Strangest Secret* by Earl Nightingale: Earl "The Voice" Nightingale was a forerunner in personal development filled. In the 1950s and '60s he had a radio show, wrote books, and recorded albums (for those who don't know that is, it's what music was recorded on made out of vinyl). The book is a transcription of the album that Earl recorded and used to train people in his insurance agency.

NOTE: Bob Proctor, who worked for Earl many years ago, became one of the top personal help speakers. You can listen to Earl and Bob on YouTube. Yes, Earl reads and teaches about *Think and Grow Rich*.

5. *The ABCs of Success* by Bob Proctor: This Is a wonderful book filled with topical lessons about success. They run from one page to five pages. It is an easy read worth your time and effort.

6. *Change Your Paradigm Change Your Life* by Bob Proctor: This is Bob's latest and is a wonderful overview on how we think, speak, and act and how we can shift our negative paradigm to a positive paradigm that will affect your life in the present and the future.

7. *Success for Dummies* by Zig Ziglar: I consider Zig to be the dean of success and prosperity. Zig was a very strong Christian who implemented principles of God for success.

8. *See You At The Top* by Zig Ziglar: This is the one that started it all for Zig as a published author. It is the premiere book for training sales people. Zig's lectures are filled with home spun humor and wisdom.

9. *The Power of Positive Thinking* by Norman Vincent Peale: Pastor of the Marble Collegiate Church, New York from 1932 until 1984, the leading Reformed Church in America. Dr. Peale was influential on TV, Radio, and his books/writings. He started *Guideposts* (the premier positive magazine) He wrote many books on positive thinking.

10. *The Success Principles* by Jack Canfield: Jack is a co-creator of the *Chicken Soup for the Soul* series and teacher and influencer for success. This is one of my *favorite* books. He has 63 chapters with 63 principles for success. As with many of these books, you may or may not read in one setting, but you will and can glean practical success principles.

11. *As a Man Thinketh* by James Allen: This is a small, compact, powerful book written in 1902 that rocked my world with a quote

from the book of Pro-Verbs 23:7, *"As a man thinketh in his heart, so he is."* Combine that with Luke 6:45 from the words of Jesus, *"Out of the abundance of the heart the mouth speaks."* I began wondering what was I I thinking and what was I saying.

12. *The Secret Kingdom* by Pat Robertson: This is the book that got me started on thinking about God's Kingdom that I could not see, and how it influence my world, what I see. He outlined principles of God and reveals God's rule on earth as it is in heaven as I say, *Yes, Lord.*

13. *Pray to Win* by Pat Boone: Pat Boone influenced my life with his book *A New Song.* This book opened my mind and eyes that there was more to my spiritual life as I sat on a pew, waiting for the train to glory. There was a deeper walk of the Holy Spirit. Pat's book reminds us that we were not created to be failures under the regime of satan (aka the d-evil), but we were created to have an intimate relationship with Jesus that affects how we live our life here on earth.

14. *The School of Greatness* by Lewis Howes: I love this book and love his audio/video podcast as Lewis interviews hundreds of movers and shaker and successful people. He is now on P.B.S.

15. *The Dream Giver* by Bruce Wilkinson: Bruce is the author of *The Prayer of Jabez, Secrets of the Vine,* and many more biblically inspirational books. *The Dream Giver* acknowledges God as the one who plants dreams in us and helps to bring them to pass. I believe that God plants desires in our hearts and brings them to pass as we delight ourselves in the Lord (make ourselves pliable to Him). (Psalm 37:4)

16. *The Red Letter Words of Jesus* by Jack Countryman: This book takes the words of Jesus and lays out devotional's that will inspire you to live a lifestyle full of faith.

17. *Act Like a Success, Think Like a Success* and *Jump* by Steve Harvey: Both of these books are very motivational. You may think, *What, Steve Harvey the comedian, the host of Family Feud, the host of various radio and T.V shows is motivational?* Well, yes he is. Steve is a born again believer who is working out his salvation from old habits to cussing. His books points me to God and to walk by faith and not by sight.

18. *How To Live Like a King's Kid* by Harold Hill: One of my favorite books about how to live life based on The Manufacture's Handbook. Harold was a logical, scientist who worked in a world of facts and not faith, until he accepted Jesus and was baptized in the Holy Spirit. There are inspiring stories after stories of God's SUPER coming on his natural as a result of prayer. Harold gets a bad rap from many *ultra-cool* Christians who turn up their noses at his belief that we live below our God-given means while they live in their fine homes, multiple cars, multiple guitars, etc. I have been in third world countries who look at the poorest people in our country and wish they had what they had. The same people look down on Joel Osteen.

19. *Your Best Life Now* by Joel Osteen: This was Joel's first book of many positive books. I love listening to Joel and read his books. No, they are not about salvation, but they are encouraging books about living out and working out your own salvation.

20. *There Is A Miracle In Your Mouth* by John Osteen: John Osteen is Joel Osteen's dad. John was a great teacher of the principles of faith. He spoke about renewing you mind with the Word of God, speak the Word of God, and act based on the Word of God. Yes, he was talking about paradigm principles before paradigms were cool. His wife is also an author who was healed of incurable cancer as a result of renewing her mind with the will of God, speaking the will of God on earth as it is in heaven, and acting out her faith. She credits of course, God, but also her husband, John, who taught her the Word of God.

21. *The Secret* by Rhonda Byrne: This was first a movie and then a book. It is where I first started thinking about The Law of Attraction, where I first heard of Bob Proctor who was in the book and movie. I would take the book and where I found things that I did not agree with I would circle, and then write in the margin of my book. For example, statements like "the universe wants to give you whatever you want" or "what you put out in the universe is what is attracted back to you." I would write that "I would rather speak to the Creator of the universe" or "I will sow to the God of the universe with an expectancy of return like seeds sown and reaping a harvest."

22. *My Utmost for His Highest* by Oswald Chambers: This book is a book of daily devotions written by, "a great evangelical mystic" and "a great expositor" but above all a "man of great spiritual stature" from Scotland. My friend and mentor gave me a copy of it back inthe '70s, and I still crack it open for wisdom to keep me balanced as I walk out Biblical Prosperity and Success, Ruminator Style.

23. *The Law of Success* by Napoleon Hill: This was the book commissioned by Andrew Carnegie which become the foundation for the book *Think and Grow Rich*.

24. *Battlefield of the Mind* by Joyce Myer: A tremendous study on the mind that produces words and is followed by actions. Combined with *Me and My Big Mouth* you have a double-punch study on words that affect our lives.

25. *The Richest Man in Babylon* by George S. Clason: a 1926 classic with financial advice that still is valid, through a collection of parables set 4,000 years ago in ancient Babylon.

26. *Giving is the Good Life* by Randy Alcorn: A powerful book that speaks of how to live a GOOD LIFE which is in essence the ABUNDANT LIFE that Jesus spoke about. The door of the Good/Abundant Life is hinged on giving.

27. *The Gospel of Wealth* by Andrew Carnegie: In the movie/comic book Spider-man, Peter Parker's Uncle Ben said, "With great power comes great responsibility." Andrew Carnegie, who in 1889 was considered to be the richest man in the world and who was the mentor to a young Napoleon Hill (who wrote *The Law of Success* that turned in to *Think and Grow Rich*. Carnegie wrote an article/book called *The Gospel of Wealth* which encouraged other wealthy, self-made rich men to accept the responsibility of meeting the needs of others.

28. The book of Pro-Verbs (Proverbs): The Holy Spirit inspired book was written by one of the wealthiest men who ever lived, Solomon. Throughout the book he wrote about borrowing, bribes, the poor, riches, and how we need to accept the responsibility of meeting the needs of those who are in need (not greed). He encouraged people to accept their personal responsibility but to help others.

GOD'S ECONOMY (PRO-VISION)

This teaching was from a request of a brother in Kenya:

"Hello pastor Rodney hope you're well there; can you share the Kingdom economy I want to get it fully."

I have found that there is no difference in people's desires anywhere in the world. This is my response—not a total study, but a thumbnail sketch of God's Economy (Pro-Vision).

ECONOMY (1) The wealth and resources of a country or region, especially in terms of the production and consumption of goods and services. (2) Careful management of available resources.

GOD'S ECONOMY: God's Provision for your life. God's Pro-Vision, Pro=Positive, Vision=Revelatory Insight

I believe that—no matter what the world economy looks like, no matter if you get an unexpected bill, no matter what the world system say about supply chain economics—if you are a believer, you have a different source. The world says that all resources are depleted, but there is no depletion of anything—merely blockages keeping the resources from you.

Back in the day there was a guru named the Maharishi Yogi, guru to the elite, especially to those rich enough to afford him. The Maharishi (remember the Three Stooges skit, mah hah...ah hah) was asked by his financial adviser (what, he had enough money to have a financial adviser?) "This will be very expensive, where will the money come from?" The Maharishi responded, "The money will come from wherever the money is."

I like that.

What is the source of our strength and supply? Philippians 4:13, 19!

In these last dazes of the Pandemic of Fear with its Systemic Sin, fueled by Systemic Hate with the Systemic Root of Bitterness wrapped around the 9.9+ billion people on Planet Earth, one of the most common fears is the fear of lack, the fear of not having enough money, wealth, stuff. This fear is not limited to non-Christians but is also prevalent in those who declare that Jesus is Lord. (Philippians 2:11)

LORD: kurios (koo'-ree-os)=From κῦρος kuros (supremacy); supreme in authority, that is, (as noun) controller; by implication Mr. (as a respectful title): - God, Lord, master, Sir.

What you are saying when you say "Jesus is Lord" is that Jesus is supreme in authority in your life. You are saying that Jesus is your Master. You are saying that Jesus is the controller, the one in control of your life. That control extends into your economy.

> *"The fool has said in their heart, there is no God."*
> ~Psalm 14:1, Psalm 51:1

The only thing worse than a fool that says in their heart there is no God, is the Christian who acts like there is no God by fearing, grumbling, complaining, whining, kvetching, moaning, and groaning about the conditions of this world, including the economy.

A current example is Christians who complain about gas prices and the current President of the United States, Joe Biden. I have gone to gas pumps when gas was in excess of $4.00 a gallon. Some people have put stickers with a picture of the President pointing to the gas price on the pump with a cartoon balloon coming out of his mouth saying, "I did that." I like to say out loud while I am pumping the gas, "My God shall supply all of my gas needs according to His riches in glory in Christ Jesus and their ain't no shortage in glory or Christ Jesus." (Philippian 4:19 with emphasis, additions, and commentary mine, Ruminator Style) Once, a man on the other pump asked me what I said, and I told him, and he responded back, "I'm going to start doing that."

All I was doing was taking control of the fear in my mind, speaking out words of faith, and acting based on a renewed mind/thought and renewed words/confession.

- ## KINGDOM ECONOMY VERSES

"Give and it shall be given unto you, good measure, pressed down, shaken together, running over shall men give into your bosom/lap/ clothing gathered to receive."

~Luke 6:38

1. What is the cause and effect when you give? (Luke 6:38)
2. Who does the giving? (Luke 6:38)

NOTE: This giving, this reciprocity is *not* just money, but time, love, etc.

3. What manner of measurement is given back to you? (Luke 6:38)
   a. _____
   b. _____
   c. _____
   d. _____

GOOD MEASURE = A fair amount

PRESSED DOWN = Tamping down to make room for more

SHAKEN TOGETHER = To make room for more, like a box of cornflakes in transit. The box looks big, but open the box it is about half full, room for more.

RUNNING OVER = This is the definition of abundance, it is overflow.

4. Who will give to you? (Luke 6:38)

NOTE: Yes, God is the giver, God is your provision, *but* God uses other things to give to you. For example, God provided meat by sending the quail, at other times, He would send a raven, at other times He would use a fish's mouth, at other times, He would multiply what was offered to Him, at other times, He would take the last meal from a needy person and then with that act of faith give a never-ending supply. The key is to *not* look to a human being to give you provision but look to God, and God will deal with the natural and supernatural to provide you your *needs* and not your *greed*.

> *"Do not be deceived, God is not mocked; for what ever a man sows this he will also reap. For the one who sows to his own flesh will from the flesh reap corruption, but the one who sows to the Spirit reap eternal life. Let us not lose heart in doing good (sowing good), for in due time we will reap IF we do not grow weary. So then, while we have opportunity, let us do good to all people, and especially to those who are of the household of the faith."*
> ~Galatians 6:7-10 emphasis and addition mine

1. Can you be deceived in the principles of sowing and reaping? (Galatians 6:7)

2. Can God be mocked? (Galatians 6:7)

3. What is the cause and effect of sowing? (Galatians 6:7)

4. What seed is included in this sowing? (Galatians 6:7)

NOTE: The word "whatever" means it could be seeds of corn or seeds of poison ivy, whatever seeds you sow. The bottom line is, if you sow seeds of corn you will get stalks of corn with multiple ears of corn that has multiple kernels of corn on it. God's economy is multiplication back to what you sow. On the negative side, if you sow poison ivy, you will get poison ivy back. The soil is no respecter of the seed. "Man who sows poison ivy should not be surprised when he gets a rash to itch." (Rodfucious Says)

5. What does the one who sows to the carnal, fleshly nature reap? (Galatians 6:8)

6. What does the one who sows to the Spirit reap? (Galatians 6:8)

NOTE: We can choose the soil that we sow our seeds into.

7. What should we not lose during our time of sowing and reaping? (Galatians 6:9)

8. When will we reap? (Galatians 6:9)

9. What is the key to reaping in due season/time? (Galatians 6:9)

NOTE: There are four seasons in the natural—winter, spring, summer, and fall. There are seasons of sowing and reaping. Two seasons/Multiple season cannot happen at the same time. Each season of reaping has a gestational time frame. Don't dig up the seed to see if it is growing. Between the point of sowing and reaping, cultivate, water, protect from animals trying to steal the seed, weed the garden.

10. What do we all have? (Galatians 6:10)

11. What should we be doing while we have the opportunity? (Galatians 6:10)

12. We are to do good to all but especially to whom should we do good? (Galatians 6:10)

NOTE: Between the point of sowing and the point of reaping, *do not* look to others to be your supply. Instead of having your hand out to other humans, find someone who has a greater need than you have and *sow/give* to them *if* you want your needs to be met.

> *"Now this is what I say, Rodney Lewis Boyd (put your name here) who sows (gives) sparingly will also reap (harvest) sparingly, and Rodney Lewis Boyd (put your name here) who sows (give) bountifully will also reap (harvest) bountifully. Each one must do just as he has purposed in his heart not grudgingly or under compulsion for God loves a cheerful (hilarious) giver. And God is able to make all grace abound to you, so that always having all sufficiency in everything, you may have an abundance for every good deed. Now He who supplies seed to the sower and bread for food will supply and multiply your seed for sowing and increase the harvest of your righteousness; you will be enriched in everything, for all liberality, which through us is producing thanksgiving to God."*
> ~2 Corinthians 9:6-8, 2 Corinthians 9:10-11 addition mine

1. What is the cause and effect of sowing sparingly/stingily? (2 Corinthians 6:7)

2. What is the cause and effect of sowing bountifully/generously? (2 Corinthians 6:7)

3. What must each one (including you) do in your sowing/giving? (2 Corinthians 6:8)

4. What should our attitude *not* be in our sowing/giving? (2 Corinthians 6:8)

5. What kind of sower/giver does God love? (2 Corinthians 6:8)

6. What is God able to do? (2 Corinthians 6:8)

7. When God's grace abounds, what to we have? (2 Corinthians 6:8)

8. *If* you have all sufficiency in everything, what do you have? (2 Corinthians 6:8)

9. What will this abundance be for? (2 Corinthians 6:8)

10. Who is the supplier of your seed? (2 Corinthians 9:10)

11. Who is the supplier of your bread? (2 Corinthians 9:10)

12. What will God do to the seed? (2 Corinthians 9:10)

13. What is the purpose for the supplying and multiplication of the seed? (2 Corinthians 9:10)

14. What will be increased with the supplied/multiplied seed? (2 Corinthians 9:10)

15. What will be enriched in? (2 Corinthians 9:11)

16. What is this enriching in everything for? (2 Corinthians 9:11)

17. What is produced? (2 Corinthians 9:11)

NOTE: Paul was taking up a collection of money for the poor in Jerusalem. He is teaching about God's economy of what happens when you sow into others—you will reap back more to sow into others. The bottom line is that you will produce the giving of thanks to God, the giver of the seed.

> *"This book of the Law (the Word of God) shall not depart from your mouth (will always be in your mouth) BUT (in contrast) you (Rodney Lewis Boyd) shall MEDITATE (think about, mull over, ruminate, ponder, mutter under your breath) on it (the Word of God) day and night (a time frame for every opportunity arises) for then (cause and effect) YOU (Rodney Lewis Boyd) will make (you do the making) your way (the way you live your life) PROSPEROUS (having enough to meet your needs, not your greed and an overflow to help others) and then you (Rodney Lewis Boyd) will have*

(cause and effect of being prosperous) GOOD (not bad) SUCCESS
(accomplishing the purposes of God in your life."
~Joshua 1:8 emphasis, additions, and commentary mine
Ruminator Style

1. What should not depart (ever leave) your mouth? (Joshua 1:8)

2. What should you be doing with this word that does not depart from your mouth? (Joshua 1:8)

3. How often should you meditate on the Word of God? (Joshua 1:8)

4. What will be when you mediated on the Word of God? (Joshua 1:8)

5. What will you do with and have with this prosperity? (Joshua 1:8)

NOTE: Prosperity and Success (not of the world or of the flesh, but of God) is directly linked to the Word of God, the Will, The Wish, The Desire of God for your life. The context is crossing over into the Promise Land (it was theirs, and it is yours to possess, but there will be obstacles, obstructions).

"Beloved, I pray that in all respects you may PROSPER and be in GOOD HEALTH, just as your soul (mind, will and emotions) PROSPERS."
~3 John 2 addition and emphasis mine

PROSPER: euodoō (yoo-od-o'-o)= to help on the road, that is, (passively) succeed in reaching; figuratively to succeed in business affairs: - (have a) prosper (-ous journey).

HEALTH: hugiainō (hoog-ee-ah'ee-no)=From G5199; to have sound health, that is, be well (in body); figuratively to be uncorrupt (true in doctrine): - be in health, (be safe and) sound, (be) whole (-some). G5199: hugiēs (hoog-ee-ace')=From the base of G837; healthy, that is, well (in body); figuratively true (in doctrine): - sound, whole. G837: auxanōowx-an'-o=A prolonged form of a primary verb;

to grow ("wax"), that is, enlarge (literally or figuratively, actively or passively): - grow (up), (give the) increase.

1. How many respects is this prayer for? (3 John 2)

2. What is the first thing that John is praying for this person? (3 John 2)

3. What is the second thing that John is praying for this person? (3 John 2)

4. What is John comparing this prosperity and health compared to? (3 John 2)

NOTE: Many theologians say that this verse is merely the opening of a letter, nothing more. I don't agree. I believe that it is an actual prayer for actual results including prosperity and health in the same way that you prosper and are healthy in your soul, in your mind (what you think), your will (what you choose based on what you think) and your emotions (the barometer of your feelings).

> *"Not that I speak (my thoughts) from (a position) of WANT, for I have learned (by experience) to be CONTENT (an emotions of calmness/peace) in WHATEVER CIRCUMSTANCE I am. I know how to get along with HUMBLE MEANS, and I also know how-to live-in PROSPERITY; in ANY and EVERY CIR-CUMSTANCE I have learned THE SECRET of being FILLED and GOING HUNGRY, both of having ABUNDANCE and SUFFERING NEED."*
> ~Philippians 4:10-12 addition and emphasis mine

1. What should we not speak from a position of? (Philippians 4:10)

NOTE: Many people believe that we should not speak what we want. We should just accept what we have, accept poverty, accept lack. I do not believe this. Let's look at the definition of what we should not speak from a position of>

WANT: husterēsis (hoos-ter'-ay-sis)=From G5302; a falling short, that is, (specifically) penury extreme poverty; destitution: (: - want. G5302: hustereō (hoos-ter-eh'-o)=From G5306; to be later, that is, (by implication) to be inferior; genitively to fall short (be deficient): - come behind (short), be destitute, fall, lack, suffer need, (be in) want, be the worse. G5306: husteros (hoos'-ter-os)

2. What should we speak from a position of? (Philippians 4:11)

3. In what circumstances should we be content? (Philippians 4:11)

NOTE: In the beatitudes (these be the attitudes that we should be having) Jesus uses the word BLESSED nine times for various circumstances. In the Amplified Bible, in Matthew 5, variations of the word BLESSED means: To be supremely happy so as to be envied by others as they see your life-joy, satisfaction, salvation REGARDLESS of your CIRCUMSTANCE.

This does not mean that you won't have circumstances, but you have learned the secret of being content, knowing that God is going to give you what you *want*.

4. In what conditions can you be content in? (Philippians 4:12)

I believe that God, through Paul, is saying *not* to speak from a position of falling short. That is a far cry from speaking about what you want, it is trusting that God will give you what you want. Until then, be *content*, knowing that God will provide.

> *"Not that I speak (my thoughts) from (a position) of falling short, extreme poverty, destitution, inferiority, deficient, lack, suffering need..."*
> ~Philippians 4:10 addition mine

> *"I can do all things through Christ Who strengthens me."*
> ~Philippians 4:13

> *"I have strength for all things in Christ Who empowers me (I am ready for anything and equal to anything through him Who infuses inner strength into me; I am self-sufficient in Christ's sufficiency)."*
> ~Philippians 4:13 addition mine

NOTE: Philippians 4:13 is in the context of God's Economy, God's Pro-Vision (Positive revelatory insights). Yes, we can have strength concerning money. There ain't no (not good English but true) shortage in God's Glory (His Presence) or His Anointed One (frequency and vibration of His anointing, that we can come into harmony with).

"And my God will liberally supply fill to the full) your every NEED/WANT according to His riches in glory (His Presence) and in Christ (the Anointed One and His anointing)."
~Philippians 4:19 emphasis, additions, commentary mine
Ruminator Style

NOTE: Philippians 4:13-19 are about the *wants* that we are not to speak from. Why? Because we live with God's Economy, provision, strength.

"The Lord is my Shepherd, I shall NOT WANT..."
~Psalm 23:1

WANT: châsêr (khaw-sare')=A primitive root; to lack; by implication to fail, want, lessen: - be abated, bereave, decrease, (cause to) fail, (have) lack, make lower, want.

"The Lord is my Shepherd I shall NOT have lack, fail, be abated, bereave, have decrease, fail made lower."
~Psalm 23:1 emphasis and addition mine

If you are *wanting*, you may need to check out your relationship with the Shepherd and *start* to speak from what you *want*.

"Our God is able to do exceedingly abundantly above all we ask or think."
~Ephesian 3:20

1. Is our God able? (Ephesians 3:20)
2. Does God just trickle down what we ask or think? (Ephesian 3:20)

3. What is Gods manner of giving us what we ask or think? (Ephesian 3:20)

- FINAL THOUGHTS...FINALLY

My questions to you are:

"What do you really *want*?"

"What are you willing to do to get what you really *want*?"

"What are the obstacles and obstructions keeping you from getting what you really *want*?"

"Who do you blame for not getting what you really *want*?"

"What are your excuses for not getting what you really *want*?"

I believe that we need to come into agreement/harmony with what God wants. His heartbeat is to give you the desires of your heart as we delight (yield our will to Him) ourselves in Him(Psalm 37:4). We have not because we ask not and when we do we ask amiss (James 4:2). We can ask whatever we wish *if* we abide in (continue in, live in, set up residence in, tabernacle in) His Word and His Word abides in (continue in, live in, set up residence in, tabernacle in) us. (John 15:7)

"Our God is able to do exceedingly abundantly above all we ask or think."

~Ephesian 3:20

1. Is our God able? (Ephesians 3:20)

2. Does God just trickle down what we ask or think? (Ephesian 3:20)

3. What is God's manner of giving us what we ask or think? (Ephesian 3:20)

   a. _____

   b. _____

   c. _____

ACKNOWLEDGEMENTS

I want to dedicate this book to the most positive person in my life, my wife of 51+ years, Brenda. When I met her back in 1969, I was a mess, and by the time we got married I got even messier. She has stuck with me in the good, bad, and ugly times. She led me to the Lord in 1970 and was with me as I learned and walked out the principles found in this book.

I want to dedicate this book to my son Phillip, and his wife Jamie. Jamie is one of the most positive things that ever happen to my son.

I want to dedicate this book to my granddaughter, the grandest thing that happened to me, Emerson Grace. When this negative world presses in on me, and I see a picture of her or she crawls up in my lap, negativity dissipates.

I want to dedicate this book to anyone who has ever sat under my teachings or read any of my books as you watched me work out these positive things in a negative world.

Last but not least, I dedicate this book to the most positive influence in my life, Jesus the Christ, the Anointed One who was and is anointed with yoke-breaking, burden-lifting, oppression-removing, healing power of the Holy Ghost and power (duNAmis, dynamic ability). Now that is positive thinking right there.

ABOUT THE AUTHOR

Rodney Boyd is first and foremost a follower of Jesus Christ. He is also a husband, dad and speech-language pathologist. Rodney holds a Master's Degree in Education with emphasis in Speech Communication and has been a practicing Speech-Language Pathologist since 1993. He holds a 2nd degree Black Belt in Wado Ryu Karate; has a passion for music of all styles; and enjoys writing, teaching the Word of God.

Rodney has been married to his high school sweetheart, Brenda, for more than 51 years and together they have one son, Phillip, a daughter-in-law, Jamie, and one granddaughter, Emerson Grace (How Sweet The Sound) Boyd.

Boyd bases his life on Colossians 3:17, "And whatever you do in word or deed, do all in the name of the Lord Jesus, giving thanks through Him to God the Father."

Connect with Rodney on line at:
www.rodneylewisboyd.com

www.ingramcontent.com/pod-product-compliance
Lightning Source LLC
Chambersburg PA
CBHW021633120626
46545CB00002B/529